WORDS, WORDS, WORDS

Teaching Vocabulary in Grades 4–12

Janet Allen

Stenhouse Publishers
York, Maine

For those in my life whose words always
make a difference

Stenhouse Publishers
www.stenhouse.com

Credit
Page 81: Sam Burchers, Max Burchers, and Bryan Burchers. *Vocabutoons, Vocabulary Cartoons:
SAT Word Power.* Copyright 1997. New Monic Books, reprinted by permission.

Library of Congress Cataloging-in-Publication Data
Allen, Janet, 1950–
        Words, words, words : teaching vocabulary in grades 4–12 / Janet Allen.
            p.   cm.
        Includes bibliographical references.
        ISBN 1-57110-085-7 (alk. paper)
        1. Vocabulary—Study and teaching. 2. Language arts. I. Title.
        LB1574.5.A45   1999
        428.1'07—dc21   98-53589
                                             CIP

Interior design by Ron Kosciak, Dragonfly Design
Cover design by Richard Hannus

Manufactured in the United States of America on acid-free paper
10 09 08 07 06 05   25 24 23 22 21 20 19 18 17 16

Contents

Acknowledgments

Many people help move a book project from an idea to the printed page. First, I would like to thank the teachers and students whose work is represented here. They have eagerly tried the vocabulary strategies and suggested improvements.

Rick Adams, *Mt. SAC Community College, San Antonio, CA*
Ann Bailey, *Jefferson Middle School, Long Beach, CA*
Barbara Barkemeyer, *Jefferson Middle School, Long Beach, CA*
Janine Brown, *Discovery Middle School, Orlando, FL*
Anne Cobb, *Carver Middle School, Orlando, FL*
Lee Corey, *Oak Ridge High School, Orlando, FL*
Nancy Demopolis-Roberts, *Dommerich Elementary School, Winter Park, FL*
Kyle Gonzalez, *Lakeview Middle School, Winter Garden, FL*
April Henderson, *Discovery Middle School, Orlando, FL*
Christine Landaker, *Carver Middle School, Orlando, FL*
Tausha Madden, *Glenridge Middle School, Orlando, FL*
Robyn Miller-Jenkins, *Gotha Middle School, Windermere, FL*
Gail Sherman, *Glenridge Middle School, Orlando, FL*
Kathie Steele, *West High School, Anchorage, AK*
Leah Wallace, *Gotha Middle School, Windermere, FL*

The people at Stenhouse always make the task of writing easier: Philippa's kindness and skillful editing keep the process moving when it might otherwise get lost; Tom's bribes for early completion of the manuscript are always a safe bet on his part; and Martha's production expertise turns my work into something I am proud to see. I am thankful for their friendship and their professionalism.

Anne Cobb has spent many hours researching, word processing, scanning, and faxing. She has shipped the manuscript from Florida to Maine so many times we were often uncertain where it actually was. She has translated the book files into several computer formats, all with cheerful hopefulness that there would finally be an end. I am thankful to call her friend and colleague.

1

Diaphragming Sentences:
A Case for Word Control

"When I use a word," Humpty Dumpty said in a rather scornful tone, "it means just what I choose it to mean—neither more nor less."

Lewis Carroll, *Through the Looking Glass*

Most of us approach language a bit like Carroll's Humpty Dumpty does. We know what we want to say but often struggle to find just the right words. The title of this chapter arises from that dilemma. Once while I was visiting Kyle Gonzalez's classroom in Orlando, one of her students boldly announced that he would like to "diaphragm that sentence."

As teachers we not only feel responsible for our own use of language, we also feel compelled to focus on vocabulary study so that our students are exposed to rich, expressive language. For secondary teachers, the academic proving ground that looms most closely for our students is the SAT, but all teachers have to deal with state- or district-mandated tests. However, most teachers have goals larger than having their students do well on those tests. They want to involve their students in productive vocabulary instruction because they know the value of well-chosen words. Unfortunately, vocabulary instruction is one of those educational arenas in which research and best practice are elusive. I think Baumann and Kameenui (1991), in their synthesis of research related to vocabulary instruction, say it best: "We know too much to say we know too little, and we know too little to say that we know enough."

For most of my teaching career I vacillated between knowing too little and knowing too much. When I began teaching, I "taught" vocabulary the same way my teachers had taught me: I assigned lists of words; asked students to look the words up in the dictionary and write them in sentences; and gave weekly vocabulary tests. Those exercises then gave way to programmed vocabulary books. My students and I worked our way through levels A–F, but it didn't take long for me to realize that these exercises didn't increase their speaking, reading, and writing language any more than looking words up in the dictionary had. Students seldom (never) gained enough in-depth word knowledge from this practice to integrate the words into their spoken or written language. These exercises did, however, keep them quiet for long periods, and I was doing what all the veteran teachers I knew were doing, so I truly wanted to believe that students were learning from this activity. In retrospect, I have to admit that it didn't matter whether students were learning or not—I simply did not know what else to do. It was my job to teach vocabulary, and if I didn't teach (or would it be more accurate to say assign?) vocabulary in the traditional ways, what would I have done instead? Many teachers today struggle with these same demons: we're supposed to be teaching vocabulary and if we don't do the traditional "assign, define, and test," what do we do instead? and if we do something different, how can we prove it's working?

For most students, finding definitions and writing those words in sentences have had little apparent impact on their word knowledge and language use. A senior in one of my classes made that point in an essay about what needed to be changed in high school English classes. Condemning the use of programmed vocabulary books, she stated, "Those are words nobody uses. Take the word *bourgeois,* for example. I'll never use that word again." And it's quite true that I seldom hear students use these words while talking with their friends or even during class discussions. In fact, when I am in schools I see students communicate almost without language—hand gestures, body language, grunts, sighs, and abbreviations seem to have taken the place of "conversation." As I listen to students, I wonder whether a single word from any teacher's vocabulary list has become integrated into their natural language. With a ninth-grade word list like that given to one student I know, which included such "highly visible" words as *mephitic, nacreous, nugatory,* and *scissile,* it makes sense that students see vocabulary study as deadly. The natural language I hear in schools today would produce the following Dolch list (words that express most of what they want to say) for adolescents:

whatever	dawg	the bomb	duh
ya—right	my bad	cool	that's bad
so?	no doubt	puh-leez	that rocks
wassup?	straight up	later	word
YO!	kid	that's phat	true-dat
as if	what it is	awesome	whaddup?
like	NOT	dissin'	borrring

My students didn't use the words I assigned from a word list. They used the words they heard on television and radio; they used words from the music they listened to; and they used the words I used with them. When all my students wanted my attention at the same time, I would laughingly accuse them of having no joy in delayed gratification. After only a few days of my joking with them like this, I heard Jennifer say to Rob, "Go sit down until I finish. Don't you have any delayed gratification?" When students asked me for a pen or pencil, I had one of two responses: "Sure you can. I seem to have a plethora of pencils today," or "Sorry. I seem to have a dearth of pencils today." Soon I heard students using those same words with each other. When it was obvious that I was pleased with students, they would say, "Are we the epitome of all the students you have?" They used and played with the language we created together—not the language I assigned.

Whenever I was in Mary Giard's first-grade classroom, I was always amazed at the level of language she used with six-year-olds;

but I also saw that in a matter of weeks those children absorbed and used that language in natural contexts. They talked about reruns in running records, strategies for reading, and self-assessment the way many students in college reading courses talk. When I returned to my high school classroom after those observations, I had a renewed passion for creating that same kind of language-rich environment. My "teaching moments" included using my natural language in ways these students had never heard before. While I joked with them about the language they used and even helped students who were kicked out of class for using "dirty words" create a list of alternatives, I saw my role as one of demonstrating a more advanced level of language. I tried not to take my language to their level but rather to bring their language to mine. When I began to see how easily students internalized the language we used together in meaningful contexts, I began to rethink the way I taught vocabulary.

This book is intended to help teachers who find themselves in a similar teaching dilemma. It shows the ways in which several teachers and I have implemented vocabulary practices that move away from decontextualized, single definitions and toward a concept-based, multilayered knowledge of words. The strategies shared here are consistent with research on how we learn new words, connect them to our existing knowledge, and retrieve them when we want to use them in reading, writing, and speaking.

A Foundation in Research

On a recent trip to California I was visiting a middle school and the teachers told me, "We're not allowed to use the word *context* anymore when we're doing vocabulary instruction." After talking with them about why they would have been given such a mandate, it occurred to me that it probably was rooted in research that cites the unreliability of context as a way to determine meaning and improve comprehension. It appears that the teaching of vocabulary has fallen into the same pit of controversy in which many other literacy practices have landed; therefore, I want to begin by sharing some of the research that has led me to develop a more specific and consistent plan for vocabulary instruction. (Appendix A lists a number of researchers and teachers whose work has influenced my thinking and practice.)

The importance of grounding our practice in research, both our own teacher research and the work of noted authorities, was brought home for me at a workshop I recently conducted, in which I asked teachers to look for common areas in teaching language arts. They came up with the following: literature, vocabulary, and writing. After we generated our list, we worked collaboratively to ground our practice in research (the form in Appendix E.1 is an excellent vehicle for structuring discussions like this). When I asked them to cite research and researchers relative to the common practices, a few teachers offered some names connected with writing and literature: Rosenblatt, Atwell, Graves, Fletcher, Romano. In the area of vocabulary, however, they drew blanks. Even though the last two decades have offered teachers a great deal of research to support changes in how we teach vocabulary, most of that research has not been translated into models for our classrooms. Most teachers therefore continue their traditional practices.

Vocabulary Research That Makes a Difference

The connection between reading comprehension and word knowledge has been clear for many years. According to Davis (1944, 1968), "vocabulary knowledge is related to and affects comprehension. The relationship between word knowledge and comprehension is unequivocal." Recent research showing the connection between word knowledge, concept development, and prior knowledge and the impact these have on reading comprehension indicates that some drastic changes in our teaching methods are warranted.

In their contribution to the *Handbook on Teaching the English Language Arts,* Baumann and Kameenui synthesize the empirical research on vocabulary instruction (their own and others') and offer their recommendations for effective practice. It is on their foundation that I have built the strategies highlighted in this book. McKeown and Beck's (1988) assertion that "word knowledge is not an all or nothing proposition. Words may be known at different levels" led me to understand that as a teacher I should not be searching for one way to teach vocabulary for all words, for all my students, for an entire year. Rather, I should be creating a language-rich environment with lots of reading, talking, and writing in which varying levels of direct instruction occur.

Beck, McCaslin, and McKeown (1980) suggest that the levels of word knowledge (unknown, acquainted, and established) dictate instructional strategies. Kameenui et al. (1982) call these levels *verbal association knowledge, partial concept knowledge,* and *full concept knowledge.* The names given these levels are not that significant; the knowledge that our vocabulary instruction must change depending on the degree to which students must be able to access a given word is. For example, a word like *run* is common enough that we want students to recognize and understand the word in multiple contexts (a run on the stock market, a run in a pair of pantyhose, a run in baseball, a press run, to run away from home); use the word in their speaking and writing; connect the word to their own lives and offer examples of its correct and incorrect use; understand subtle shades in the word's meaning; and generate effective contexts to help others understand the word. Conversely, encountering a word like *lodestone* in our science books, we might simply say, "This is a rock with magnetic properties." Later, if we encounter the word *lodestone* again in a story about someone with a magnetic personality, we would help students recognize how the meaning transferred from a physical property to a personality trait.

Knowing I could teach words at different levels depending on their importance, frequency, and applicability in other contexts forced me to reexamine how we attempt to learn new words. I first needed to decide whether to treat a word/concept as incidental, offer mediated support, or provide direct instruction. To help me do this, I developed a series of ten questions:

1. Which words are most important to understanding the text?
2. How much prior knowledge will students have about this word or its related concept?
3. Is the word encountered frequently?
4. Does the word have multiple meanings (is it polysemous)?
5. Is the concept significant and does it therefore require preteaching?
6. Which words can be figured out from the context?
7. Are there words that could be grouped together to enhance understanding a concept?
8. What strategies could I employ to help students integrate the concept (and related words) into their lives?
9. How can I make repeated exposures to the word/concept productive *and* enjoyable?
10. How can I help students use the word/concept in meaningful ways in multiple contexts?

These questions helped me plan vocabulary instruction at the beginning of a thematic unit or before starting the shared reading of a novel. My first step was to determine which words were critical to understanding the text. I then had to decide which of those critical words could be connected to students' prior knowledge or learned through context and which would have to be bridged with direct instruction. For words that needed bridging, I then had to decide what form that bridging would take: teaching strategy lessons, suggesting concept connections, exploring multiple meanings, and/or introducing activities that provided repetition and integration into students' lives.

Given the time teachers spend asking students to find and give back definitions in the hope that it will improve reading comprehension, it is especially important to highlight research on the connection between definitional information and comprehension. Baumann and Kameenui (1991) cite several research studies that confirm the relative ineffectiveness of the definitional approach. Kameenui et al. (1982) state that "training in definitions or synonyms only has not improved students' understanding of texts that contain those words." Stahl and Fairbanks (1986) concur: "Methods that provided only definitional information about each to-be-learned word did not produce a reliable effect on comprehension. Also, drill-and-practice methods, which involve multiple repetitions of the same type of information about a target word using only associative processing, did not appear to have reliable effects on comprehension." The implication for teaching is strong: it takes more than definitional knowledge to know a word, and we have to know words in order to identify them in multiple reading and listening contexts and use them in our speaking and writing.

This focus on looking words up in the dictionary often occurs before a text is read. In a language arts class in which the whole class is studying the same novel, it is not unusual for the teacher to have created a list of vocabulary words to accompany every chapter. When I was supervising student interns, one of my students asked me for some good ideas for teaching vocabulary. When I reminded her that we had studied many ways to teach students new words, she said she couldn't use any of them because they took too much time. When I asked why her students needed to learn the words so quickly, she replied, "They have over one hundred words to learn in the first three chapters of the novel." I had the sinking feeling that it would take a long, long time for students to read a novel that really did contain over one hundred unknown words in the first three chapters! In *Reading in Junior Classes,* Simpson gives an excellent reason for abandoning the prevalent practice of asking students to look up extensive lists of words in advance. "Teaching words ahead . . . makes children unwilling to face the hazard of a new book: in short, teaching words ahead produces dependent rather than independent readers."

Nagy et al. (1987) estimate that students learn approximately three thousand new words per year. While estimates vary about the number of words students know or should know (usually because the definition of what it means to know a word varies), there is no doubt that students need to encounter many words in order to make significant gains in the number of words they know. Nagy et al. also say that if students do a modest amount of reading (which they define as three thousand words per day), they will encounter ten thousand different unknown words in a year. When such reading is combined with new words encountered through conversation, television, movies, radio, and computer programs, multiple opportunities exist for students to learn new words. In fact, Nagy et al. estimate that from 25 to 50 percent of annual vocabulary growth can be attributed to incidental learning from context while reading. So, while single context only is an unreliable method of learning new words, extensive reading, the context of longer texts, multiple exposures to the same word, and instruction in learning from context lead to increased comprehension.

Why Teach Vocabulary?

Once I realized that the traditional methods I was using for vocabulary instruction were ineffective, I stopped teaching vocabulary for several years. I realized that my students were learning lots of words from the considerable amount of reading we did and from our classroom talk, but I wasn't supporting that indirect word learning with explicit vocabulary instruction. Since I had no idea what to do to meet the goals I had for helping my students increase their comprehension and become independent word learners, I did the only thing that I knew was working: I assigned more shared and independent reading. I believed that students would actually learn more new words from reading than anything I could do, and so I simply gave them more time to read.

I don't feel any guilt over my lack of systematic vocabulary instruction during those years, because there is much research indicating that reading is the single most important factor in increased word knowledge (Anderson and Nagy 1991; Baumann and Kameenui 1991). If I had to err, I'm glad I erred on the side of increasing reading time and abandoning what wasn't working. I finally discovered, however, that the secondary learners in my classroom needed extensive reading *and* direct instruction in word-learning strategies in order to become fluent, independent readers. Baker, Simmons, and Kameenui, in a technical report entitled *Vocabulary Acquisition: Curricular and Instructional Implications for Diverse Learners* (1995a), support my findings: "Students with poor vocabularies, including diverse learners, need strong and systematic educational support to become successful independent word learners" (7). I realized that the fluent readers in my classroom had internalized ways to learn new words and connect them to future reading. Those readers who were struggling needed to spend a lot of time reading, but they also needed me to show them how readers make sense out of unknown words. Shared reading, defined by Mooney (1990) as "eyes past print with voice support," became the means whereby I could help students both learn new words and develop in-depth knowledge of words they knew only in a single context. As I read to the students while they followed along in individual copies of the text, students used Post-its to mark words for later discussion. I interrupted the reading only if students appeared to be lost because of an unknown word. During prereading and postreading, however, I supported students' developing word knowledge in a variety of ways:

- Repeated words in varied contexts.
- Described words.
- Supported words with visuals.
- Connected words to students' lives.

- Extended words with anecdotes.
- Made associations.
- Gave definitions.
- Compared and contrasted.
- Questioned.
- Charted characteristics.
- Rephrased sentences.
- Analyzed structure.
- Provided tactile examples.
- Gave examples of correct and incorrect usage.

I found at least five reasons I needed to incorporate this type of direct vocabulary instruction: to increase reading comprehension; to develop knowledge of new concepts; to improve range and specificity in writing; to help students communicate more effectively; and to develop deeper understanding of words and concepts of which they were partially aware. The importance of this planned vocabulary instruction in all content areas is supported by Baker, Simmons, and Kameenui (1995b): "Vocabulary acquisition is crucial to academic development. Not only do students need a rich body of word knowledge to succeed in basic skill areas, they also need a specialized vocabulary to learn content area material" (35). It is therefore necessary for all content area teachers to know and use effective strategies for helping students understand both common words used in uncommon ways and specialized vocabulary.

From Research to Practice

Knowing what didn't work was easy. Finding and reading the research related to word knowledge was also not very difficult. Knowing how to implement that research in effective, interesting ways turned out to be the hard part. Baumann and Kameenui (1991) express the same dilemma: "It was relatively easy to express what we know and don't know about vocabulary acquisition and what works and does not work in vocabulary instruction. It was quite another matter to translate this knowledge into sound pedagogy." As I developed teaching strategies for implementing direct vocabulary instruction into a balanced literacy program, I decided to use Baker, Simmons, and Kameenui's (1995a) guidelines for vocabulary learning. They characterize these instructional methods as "big ideas for making words/concepts more explicit and employable." They include conspicuous strategies, strategic integration, mediated scaffolding, primed background knowledge, and judicious review. In order to translate those "big ideas" into specific instruction in my classroom I needed to understand each of Kameenui's levels of word knowledge (verbal association, partial concept knowledge, and full concept knowledge) and determine ways that the "big ideas" could help me help students acquire these three levels of knowledge.

Since graphics help me look at ways to test and implement research, I created Figure 1.1 as a way for me to visualize the three levels and associate them with information about what students need at each level. At the verbal association (incidental) level, students encounter everyday words as well as words that have single definitional contexts in their current language repertoire. At the partial concept (mediated) level, students examine words that have deeper, multiple meanings. At the full concept (explicit) level, students study important words in ways that lead them to still deeper levels of understanding: multiple contexts, word analysis, connections to their lives and the world.

I also wanted to make sure that Nagy's (1988) three properties of effective vocabulary instruction (integration, repetition, and meaningful use) were present at all three levels. At the verbal association level, I needed to offer time for—and model—the wide and varied reading that would help students learn words in context. At the partial concept level, I offered support by demonstrating various strategies for getting

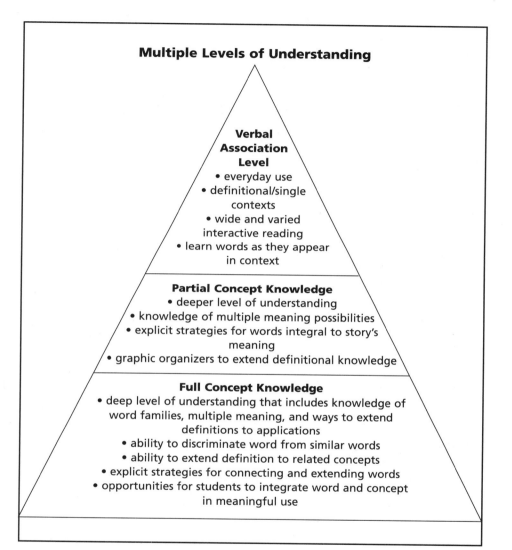

Multiple Levels of Understanding

Verbal Association Level
• everyday use
• definitional/single contexts
• wide and varied interactive reading
• learn words as they appear in context

Partial Concept Knowledge
• deeper level of understanding
• knowledge of multiple meaning possibilities
• explicit strategies for words integral to story's meaning
• graphic organizers to extend definitional knowledge

Full Concept Knowledge
• deep level of understanding that includes knowledge of word families, multiple meaning, and ways to extend definitions to applications
• ability to discriminate word from similar words
• ability to extend definition to related concepts
• explicit strategies for connecting and extending words
• opportunities for students to integrate word and concept in meaningful use

Figure 1.1

meaning from words that are integral to the story's meaning. Baker, Simmons, and Kameenui (1995a) stress that readers don't need to know all definitions of a word in order to use it successfully. They just need to know meanings that parallel the expected usage. (This is a good place to use graphic organizers to help students extend the partial knowledge they might have.) At the full concept level, I needed to introduce activities that helped my students discriminate more subtle shades of meaning, connect and extend words, and integrate words and concepts into meaningful use.

In my classroom and the classrooms of the other teachers who have contributed ideas to this book, word-learning opportunities begin with significant amounts of reading; from this reading, extensive knowledge of words and opportunities for mediated and explicit instruction emerge. In James Howe's *The Watcher*, the main character has attained the kind of independent love of language that is our goal as teachers:

> *Amidst.*
>
> The word grabbed her attention, as words will do to those who love them, and held her in its power. It wasn't the word alone, but the fact that she had *thought* it, had actually *used* it in a sentence in her own private thoughts, that so fascinated her she sat unable to move.
>
> *Here I am amidst their possessions.*
>
> It was so literary, so antiquated, that word. How in the world had it found a place in her head?
>
> *Silly girl,* she said to herself, *your head is the perfect place for words nobody else uses.*
>
> *Your head,* she thought, *is an orphanage for words.*

Larger Contexts: Meaningful, Connected, and Rich Uses of Language

My language is changing. I don't understand it. I read all those books and then I find these words just coming out of my mouth. I don't even know where they come from.

Sarah, 10th grade

The day Sarah came running into the room exclaiming that she was "possessed by books," I thought she was talking about how much time she was spending reading now that she was hooked as a reader. Although that may have been part of what she meant, she was really saying that she was now recognizing and using words that were not "her own words"—words, phrases, and idioms I recognized from the books she was reading during both shared and independent reading. For example, after we read *The Crucible,* Sarah wrote in her journal, about a boy she liked: "I think softly on him from time to time." Those were John Proctor's words about Abigail Williams. Another day, Sarah said, "I think about him sinking his teeth into my milky, white flesh." (We probably don't want to explore the titles she was reading at that time.)

Sarah is an example of what Nagy et al. (1985) document in their research about incidental learning of vocabulary: "Massive vocabulary growth seems to occur without much help from teachers." One of the ways this occurs is through the extensive amount of reading that occurs in a balanced literacy program: read-alouds and shared, guided, and independent reading (these reading approaches are defined in Chapter 4). When reading selections for each of these approaches cover a variety of writing, fiction and nonfiction, opportunities for vocabulary growth happen many times over the course of each week.

This, of course, presupposes that students actually learn words from context, and there are many who see this as an unreliable source of definitional information. Baumann and Kameenui (1991) summarize the research related to context in the following three points:

1. Context clues are relatively ineffective means for inferring the meaning of specific words.
2. Students are more apt to learn specific new vocabulary when definitional information is combined with contextual clues than when contextual analysis is used in isolation.
3. Research on teaching contextual analysis as a transferable and generalizable strategy for word learning is promising but limited.

Recognizing the limitations of context as an avenue of word knowledge, let's look at why using context is seen as unreliable and how we can overcome some of that unreliability.

Why Not Context?

For most of my teaching career, the only advice I had for students who encountered a word they didn't know was to figure it out from the context. In *It's Never Too Late* (1995, 102–104), I discuss the basis of my singular focus: when I asked my high school students how they learned new words, they told me they knew only two ways, look it up and sound it out in the sentence. Research studies have shown that these strategies are an unreliable source of information if we define context simply as the sentence in which we find the unknown word. There is seldom enough information in a single sentence to help students assimilate the word. The context appears to be helpful only if one already knows the meaning of the word. The examples below illustrate this point:

a.   Her flightiness caused her to end up without resources.
b.   Although Monica's actions were subdued, her sister's were frenzied.

In the first example, someone who knows a definition for flightiness that includes irresponsibility would connect irresponsibility to ending up without resources. If one doesn't know this definition, there are lots of reasons someone might end up without resources—loss of a job, illness, gambling, bad luck, moving—and flightiness could mean any one of them. In fact, when I use this example with students, they immediately connect losing resources with moving around a lot, because of the word *flight* in *flightiness*. In the second example, if *subdued* is the word students are trying to define, they would have to know the word *frenzied* (and vice versa) to make even a guess at the contrasting definition. The contexts given in these two examples are considered "lean," because there is not enough information to help learners define the target words. Contrast this lean context with a rich context like this one, found in the secondary social studies textbook *America's Past and Promise* (Mason et al. 1995, 322) in a passage about the Lewis and Clark expedition:

> In Jefferson's map-lined study, he and Lewis began to plan the trip. They called it the Corps of Discovery. ("Corps," pronounced "core," means a group of people acting together.)

Here readers are given a pronunciation, an easily understood definition, and a common word for an uncommon one (*trip* for *expedition*).

Graves and Graves (1994) make a distinction between teaching vocabulary and teaching concept. Teaching vocabulary is teaching new labels for familiar concepts. For example, if our students already know the concept *fair/unfair*, then we are teaching vocabulary when we connect words like *discrimination, bias,* and *stereotyping* to that concept. On the other hand, if a concept totally unknown to the student is to be studied, then more time will be required to develop a meaningful understanding. For example, if the concept *faithfulness* is new to students, a teacher would have to design several reading, writing, thinking, and exploring activities to help them understand it. Once an understanding of the concept is in place, vocabulary words like *loyalty, steadfast,* and *commitment* could then be connected to it. Vocabulary researchers believe that concept-based vocabulary instruction has the most lasting impact.

When we are planning vocabulary instruction, the context helps us decide whether or not we have to give explicit or mediated instruction. If the context is specific enough for students to recognize, define, or make sense of the word and if there is enough information to allow students to connect the word to their background knowledge, no additional instruction is necessary. If not, the word or concept requires teacher mediation. The form in Appendix E.2 can be used by teachers who are preparing a shared reading of a novel. Most teachers highlight words they believe students need to know. After examining which words have a lean context and which have a rich context, a teacher can make one list of words (those with a rich context) that will simply be referenced during reading and another list of words that are critical to the text but have a lean context and so will need some explicit instruction.

Adams and Cerqui's *Effective Vocabulary Instruction* (1989) suggests a helpful way to determine which words students will not be able to learn from context. Let's work through an example. Figure 2.1 lists words that are critical to the shared reading of John Christopher's novel *The White Mountains.* As I read each word orally, students wrote the word in the column that best described their knowledge of the word. (Most students put *pretext* in the "Don't know at all" column, and many students put *contraption* in the "I think I know the meaning" column.) The words that appeared most often in the "Don't know at

E.3 How Well Do I Know These Words?

Title: _The White Mountains_

Figure 2.1

Directions: First, read the words at the bottom of the page silently. After you read each one, write the words from the bottom of this page in the column that best describes what you know about each one.

Don't know at all	Have seen or heard—don't know meaning	I think I know the meaning	I know a meaning

pretext   converse   envision
taciturn   acquiescence   soothe
contraption   ludicrous   confirmation
       resourceful

Copyright © 1999 Janet Allen. *Words, Words, Words.* Stenhouse Publishers.

all" column were the ones I needed to teach in a strategy lesson. However, I quickly realized that this graphic organizer ignored two critical pieces of information: context and talk that might activate background knowledge. So I added another organizer (Figure 2.2). This time I read each word in context (see Figure 2.3). After I read the word and the sentence in which the word was used, I gave students the opportunity to discuss the word, sentence, and possible meanings with a partner. After a minute, students would write the word in the first column if they still needed help or in the second or third columns depend-

E.4 How Well Do I Know These Words?

Title: _The White Mountains_

Figure 2.2

Directions: As I read the words listed below in the context of the story, you and your partner should decide if you know a meaning for the word that would fit the context. List the word, and your guess for the meaning of the word if you think or know that you know it, under the appropriate column.

I still need help finding a meaning for this word	I think I know the meaning	I know a meaning
pretext	converse	envision
taciturn	acquiescence	soothe
contraption	ludicrous	confirmation
	resourceful	

Copyright © 1999 Janet Allen, *Words, Words, Words*. Stenhouse Publishers.

ing on their knowledge of the word in this context. If students listed the word in the "I think I know" or "I know" columns, they also jotted down possible definitions and we discussed them. The words that appeared in the "I still need help" column became "the word for the day" and received more in-depth study (these strategies are described in Chapter 3).

Obviously, we shouldn't ignore context entirely. Nagy et al. (1987) provide ample support for teaching students how to use context. They found that students who read grade-level texts under natural conditions have about a one-twentieth chance of learning meaning from

---

Part II: Words I Know: *The White Mountains*

Directions: Sit with a partner and look at the underlined word as I read the sentence in which we find the word in the novel *The White Mountains*. After hearing the sentence, you and your partner now need to decide if you know a meaning for the word, think you know the meaning for the word, or still need some help in finding a meaning.

1. (27) He hoped he would hear no more such reports, and I was not to go into the Vagrant House on any <u>pretext.</u>
2. (28) He that hath no friend can travel at his own pace, and pause, when he chooses, for a few minutes to <u>converse.</u>
3. (36) Cities were destroyed like anthills, and millions on millions were killed or starved to death. Millions . . . I tried to <u>envision</u> it, but I could not.
4. (47) My Uncle Ralph, on the other hand, was a gloomy and <u>taciturn</u> man, who had been willing—perhaps relieved—to let his son go to another's home.
5. (49–50) I said, "You do as you like, I'm lying up."
   He shrugged. "We'll stay here if you say so."
   His ready <u>acquiescence</u> did not <u>soothe</u> me.
6. (72) He thrust his head forward, the <u>contraption</u> on his nose looking even more <u>ludicrous,</u> and said, "You wish to go to the boat? I can still help."
7. (74) I looked at Henry, but I scarcely needed *confirmation.* Someone whom we already know to be *resourceful,* who knows the country and the language. It was almost too good to be true.

Figure 2.3

context. Further, if average fifth graders spend about twenty-five minutes a day reading, they encounter about twenty thousand unfamiliar words. If one-twentieth of those words can be figured out from context, they learn about a thousand new words per year from that strategy; hardly an insignificant amount! In fact, Anderson et al. (1986), in their study of children in grades 2 through 5, found that the amount of time spent reading was the best predictor of vocabulary growth. Therefore, I'm not willing to abandon the use of context; rather, I suggest we expand our teaching of what it means to use context and increase the amount of time students spend reading.

Although I repeated hundreds of times, "Use the context," it wasn't until my last two years of teaching that I showed students what that meant, by demonstrating the "word attack" strategies confident readers use as they read. Figure 2.4 illustrates that process as I understand it. When readers come upon a word that seems unfamiliar, they ask themselves two questions: *Do I know the word?* and *Do I need to know the word?* If they know the word, they ask themselves how they know the word (in what context) and if the way they know the word is helpful in this context. In other words, fluent readers are constantly asking themselves whether they need to refine the definitions they carry in their heads when they encounter a known word used in an unknown way. On the other hand, if they don't know the word, they ask themselves whether they need to know the word in order to continue reading and,

Figure 2.4

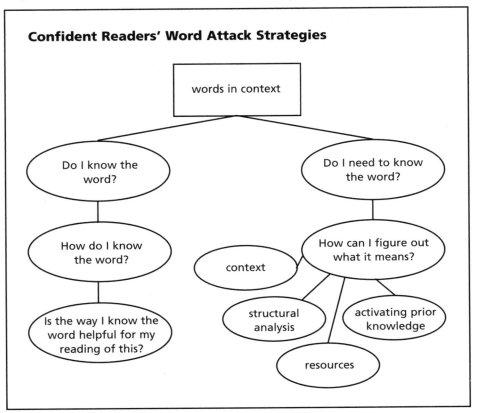

if they do, how can they go about figuring out a meaning. Proficient readers determine unknown words in a variety of ways: using context, analyzing the structure of the word, activating prior knowledge, and using available resources. Each of these strategies can be modeled and supported within the context of shared reading. After I had used these supported strategies with my students over the course of the year, they were able to list twelve different ways they attacked new words:

1. Look at the word in relation to the sentence.
2. Look the word up in the dictionary and see if any meanings fit the sentence.
3. Ask the teacher.
4. Sound it out.
5. Read the sentence again.
6. Look at the beginning of the sentence again.
7. Look for other key words in the sentence that might tell you the meaning.
8. Think what makes sense.
9. Ask a friend to read the sentence to you.
10. Read around the word and then go back again.
11. Look at the picture if there is one.
12. Skip it if you don't need to know it.

Teaching Students How to Attack Words

First, teachers should demonstrate how they use context as one of several strategies for determining the meaning of unfamiliar words. Talking through the process (thinking aloud) gives students the opportunity to hold the teacher's thought processes up as a mirror for their own thinking. Let's imagine we encounter the word *agrizoophobia* in the sentence "Marcia's agrizoophobia made her opt for a trip to the beach rather than a visit to Lion Country Safari on a recent trip to West Palm Beach." Thinking aloud,

I could make some guesses about what *agrizoophobia* means based on several cues I receive as I read the word and the sentence. I immediately recognize the word *phobia,* which means fear of something. Knowing that, I then discriminate between the two options Marcia had: going to the beach or to Lion Country Safari. I know that the beach offers sun, sand, shells, people, and water sports, while Lion Country Safari probably offers sun, people, and wild animals. Obviously Marcia feared something, and when I think of the word *zoo,* I think of wild animals, so I would guess that *agrizoophobia* may mean fear of wild animals. In order to figure out the meaning I used the context, structural analysis of the word, and my background knowledge.

When I talked with students about context, the only reference point I ever used was the surrounding text of the sentence. As I have worked through my understanding of context, I now see it in a much larger sense. Contextual clues come in two varieties: semantic/syntactic (Figure 2.5) and typographic (Figure 2.6). Semantic and syntactic

Figure 2.5

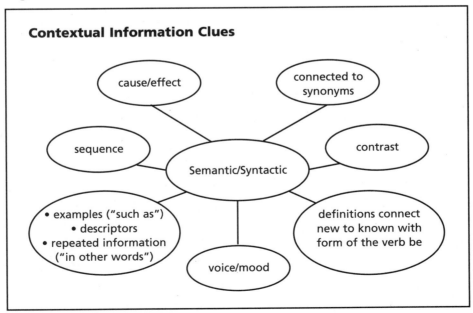

clues (knowledge of words and knowledge of structure) help readers predict words in several ways. Knowing that a larger piece of text is discussing cause and effect helps readers anticipate cue words like *motivation, impetus,* or *consequence.* If an essay is designed to show sequence, we might anticipate a word like *chronologically;* if it is a contrast essay, we can expect a word like *conversely.* Helping students understand semantic/syntactic clues in material ranging from the expository text commonly found in textbooks (cause and effect, sequence, comparison/contrast, problem/solution, and definition) to the nuances of voice and mood more commonly found in fiction and poetry is easily done if their reading is varied and language-rich. For example, in a middle school classroom, books teachers and students share together might include Mooney's historical fiction about the Rumanian revolution, *The Voices of Silence;* Haddix's journal, *Don't You Dare Read This, Mrs. Dunphrey,* which she wrote as an assignment for an English class; word-origin books like Funk's *Horsefeathers and Other*

Figure 2.6

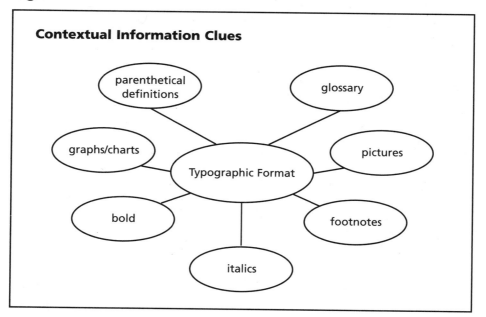

Curious Words and Hill and Ottchen's *Shakespeare's Insults: Educating Your Wit;* pictures books like *The High Rise Glorious Skittle Skat Roarious Sky Pie Angel Food Cake;* and nonfiction like Murphy's *The Great Fire* and *The World Almanac for Kids 1998.* This range of reading from realistic to historical fiction, from reference books to picture books, challenges students to use a variety of strategies for decoding new words that they encounter in unfamiliar contexts. Teachers have the opportunity to show students not only how semantic and syntactic cues help readers, but also how typographic cues such as pictures, graphs, charts, glossaries, and footnotes aid readers in understanding new words. Reading engaging books helps students connect individual words with larger concepts related to events and phenomena.

How Janine Brown Teaches Multiple Context Clues in Her Middle School Classroom

"It may seem odd that direct, explicit instruction is necessary for students to understand typographical and syntactic/semantic aids. For many teachers, myself included, these aids are so obvious that we assume our students are using them as tools to unlock meaning. This year I was teaching the SQ3R method (survey, question, read, respond, and review—Robinson 1961) as a comprehension tool. I used a selection in my literature text that discussed the differences between owl and human eyes (from *"owls,"* by Herbert Spencer Zim). I purposely chose that piece because I knew it would be easy to grasp and appropriate for introducing the SQ3R method. I gave each student a handout that detailed some of the ways an author defines words in context, and I challenged my students to find instances in the text that followed the patterns listed on the handout.

"While my students were scouring the piece for context clues, I connected my computer to a TV screen so everyone could see what I was doing. As each student pointed out how the author used a context clue, I paraphrased what the student was saying and typed the comment, followed by the student's name, onto the screen.

"Participation abounded! Not only were my students eager to discover these clues, they were pleased to see their names on television! Sometimes a student would identify a clue, but her explanation would be wrong or unclear and another student would step in to say that the clue actually followed a different pattern. The challenge of discovering these clues led to a very productive class. When the session was over, I printed a copy of our class notes for each student.

"I still didn't know whether students would transfer these strategies to a different text so I decided to test their prowess using a fiction piece. My students instantly keyed in on the highlighted glossary words but then went to work discovering the more subtle context clues and identifying which method the author was using to define new vocabulary in context. I shouldn't have been surprised that they were so eager and enthusiastic. A discussion even erupted about the differences between fiction and nonfiction context clues. A teachable moment!"

Nagy (1988) has stated that "what is needed to produce vocabulary growth is not more vocabulary instruction, but more reading." Janine's narration of the events in her classroom illustrates a way that teachers can infuse a literacy workshop with conspicuous strategy instruction. Students were able to discover and discuss concrete and fairly obvious typographical context clues such as charts, pictures, glossary words, and references. With assistance from Janine, they were also able to find the more subtle semantic context clues such as cause-and-effect signifiers (*if/then*) and comparison/contrast words (*alike, different, versus*). Janine's lesson allowed her to make these strategies conspicuous so her students could examine the clues and look at the ways authors use these cue words to help them understand text. Sequence cues like *first, next,* and *finally* helped Janine's students recognize and understand other, more difficult, sequence cues like *initially, subsequently,* and *ultimately*.

As students have opportunities to see, hear, and discuss words in contexts that are rich and meaningful, language comes alive for them. While some of this word learning could be classified as incidental during independent reading, it is intentional and often explicit during shared and guided reading. The following dialogue occurred while Kyle Gonzalez's middle school students were discussing Beatrice Sparks's *It Happened to Nancy* with a science teacher, Judith Johnson. Kyle had read this book (the diary of a young girl who contracts and dies from AIDS) as a shared reading and the students were now looking at the science behind the story.

JOHNSON: So, what has happened in this book?

STUDENTS: She got HIV.

STUDENT: She got AIDS 'cause it was contagious.

JOHNSON: What do I mean if I say something is contagious?

STUDENTS: Something catching—colds, chicken pox. Can't be around someone—you catch their germs.

JOHNSON: How do those germs get from one person to another?

STUDENTS: Touching, STDs, saliva, toilet seats, bacteria.

JOHNSON: Bacteria. What is the difference between bacteria and viruses? (*Students are uncertain*) We're going to do a simulation to see if we can figure out the difference between these words. Does anyone know what that is?

STUDENTS: Artificial holograms. Stuff that might be dangerous—we can sort of pretend. Work in simulators. (*Dr. Johnson then takes the students through a simulation see Jones 1993 that helps them understand the words generated in their discussion. In the activity, the students exchange a base solution, some of which is contaminated, with two other students and then test the fluid in their vial for contamination infection.*)

Baker, Simmons, and Kameenui's (1995b) highlight the importance of this kind of reciprocal support: "The relation between reading comprehension and vocabulary knowledge is strong and unequivocal. Although the causal direction of the relation is not understood clearly, there is evidence that the relation is largely reciprocal."

This exploration of language related to a text can occur after the reading (as it did in the example from Kyle's classroom) or before. Let's look at some prereading strategies. The students in a middle school in Daytona Beach were reading Konigsburg's *From the Mixed-Up Files of Mrs. Basil E. Frankweiler.* Their teachers felt that the students would understand the story better if they understood Claudia's fascination with language and correct words. Three of several vocabulary tasks are shown in Figure 2.7. Each of these tasks asks students actively to examine and construct language before reading certain passages in the novel. Students not only learned Claudia's language but also connected this language to that used by their friends and family members.

The above examples highlight language internalized from fiction, but it is extremely important that the reading experiences in a balanced literacy program include nonfiction as well. Sutherland and Arbuthnot in *Children and Books* (1991), stress this point: "If there is one trait that is common to children of all ages, of all backgrounds, of all ethnic groups, it is curiosity. Children read information books to satisfy that curiosity, whether their books have been chosen to answer questions on a particular subject or to fulfill a desire for broader knowledge" (497). Nonfiction satisfies curiosity while expanding vocabulary, building content knowledge, creating background knowledge to supplement or support the material in textbooks, and familiarizing readers with expository text structures commonly found in technical manuals, textbooks, and standardized tests. When students read a variety of genres, they learn to use semantic, syntactic, and typographic cues in diverse contexts. Chapter 4 highlights informational texts in each content area that can be used to expand subject-area knowledge either in conjunction with or in place of textbook instruction.

Vocabulary Task:

From the Mixed-Up Files of Mrs. Basil E. Frankweiler

"Quiet Words"

As Claudia and Jamie are trying to go to sleep (p. 46), Claudia changes her thoughts so that it will be easier for her to fall asleep. "Instead of oxygen and stress, Claudia thought now of hushed and quiet words: glide, fur, banana, peace."

Language Task: Interview all of the students in this class and ask each student to give you at least one example of his/her "hushed and quiet words." Then, ask several adults (teacher, parents, friends, etc.) to do the same thing. Compare the two lists. Are they the same or different?

"If you can't say anything nice . . ."

There is a saying in our culture that tells us, "If you can't say anything nice, don't say anything at all." Euphemisms are inoffensive ways of saying things that might be offensive. On page 151, Claudia tries to teach Jamie about euphemisms when they are discussing Mrs. Frankweiler's dead husband:

"Her husband is dead. You can't be a mother without a husband."

Claudia poked Jamie. "Never call people *dead;* it makes others feel bad. Say 'deceased' or 'passed away.'"

Language Task: Make a list of offensive words that you hear in your world (school, friends, home, etc.) and then try to find a euphemism for each of those terms. Remember, your goal is to find "nice" ways to communicate!

"Languaging"

Learning about language can be fun *and* it can also make the difference between understanding the author's message to the reader and being lost in unknown words or phrases. Some of the words or phrases in *From the Mixed-Up Files of Mrs. Basil E. Frankweiler* may be new to us because it is language that we are not used to using. Languaging is a way to make those words and phrases part of our "working vocabulary."

Language Task: (16) "fiscal week"

Find a resource who can explain to you what a fiscal week/year is in the business sense of the word. Now, Claudia is not talking about business when she uses this phrase. What is she talking about? How does she connect her responsibility for a "fiscal week" to the business meaning of the word?

Figure 2.7

Aldous Huxley once said, "Words form the thread on which we string our experiences." If words do indeed form the thread, then reading weaves those threads together in ways that invite each of us to find beauty in the patterns that are created. I was recently in a school where a teacher told me how awful she felt because she had stopped reading with her students every day, in order to get them ready for the vocabulary portion of their state-mandated standardized reading tests. She was teaching suffixes and roots and requiring students to memorize lists of words. Some students were sleeping; others were talking; some were writing notes; a few were copying items from the overhead projector. On a previous visit I'd seen this same class excitedly talking about and creating words during their reading of Philbrick's *Freak the Mighty.* The teacher remarked that although she was working hard to get the students to increase their vocabulary, each day she felt they were taking one step forward and two back. When I mentioned the contrast in behavior and interest between my two visits, she said one of her students had recently made the same point. He had stopped her midlesson one day and said, "Why don't we study any good words like the ones we just learned when we read *Freak the Mighty*?" Why indeed?

So often our goals are good and true, but the furor of educational pressures makes us abandon the very things that would help us reach those goals. None of the strategies in this book, nor all of them combined, will take the place of the wealth of words learned in a strong reading program that includes time for you to read to your students, time for them to read with you and other students, and time for them to read self-selected books independently. This reading forms the larger context for any word study a teacher may choose to do.

Alternatives to, Look It Up in the Dictionary!

A definition is the enclosing of a wilderness of idea within a wall of words.

Samuel Butler

Dictionaries and programmed vocabulary books have been the mainstay of vocabulary instruction in language arts classrooms for many years. I spent most of my career telling students, "Look it up in the dictionary," when they asked me what a word meant. I handed out lists of words and had students copy definitions and write the words in sentences. Still they didn't know the words. They asked me which definition to copy from the dictionary. I told them to copy the one that made sense, the one that fit the context. They looked at me as if I were an alien and asked, "Can we copy the shortest one?" None of the definitions made sense to them. Often they didn't even understand the words used in the definitions. When I gave a test in which the students had to match words with definitions, they had a fit if I didn't use the same definition they had copied. It mattered little to them that I had chosen definitions that made sense in the context of what we were reading. They had not internalized a meaning during our reading. At best, they knew only the meaning they copied. Often they didn't even know that meaning.

Let's look at some of the reasons that simply looking up words in a dictionary and copying them down doesn't work.

- The definition can be inaccurate for the geographic location in which you live. For example, when I look the word *mess* up in the dictionary, one definition is "disorderly mass." Yet when I was conducting a workshop in North Carolina and we had spent a particularly enjoyable day together, the teachers said to me, "Janet, you're a mess!" I immediately looked at my clothing to see whether I had spilled food or buttoned my jacket incorrectly. At home in Maine, those would have been my first meaning options in that situation. Other options would have included a "mess" of trout or a "mess" of fiddleheads, but I knew they weren't calling me a quantity of food. Clearly I didn't understand their definition of mess. When they explained that for them the term meant funny and full of life, I felt complimented, but there was nothing in my prior understanding of the word to indicate it was meant positively.

- The dictionary definition may not be understandable if applied literally. We could each come up with a four-letter synonym for *floozy*. But if we look *floozy* up in the dictionary, we find it defined as "a slovenly or vulgar woman." Just for fantasy's sake, pretend you have students who look up the words they don't know in a dictionary. They would then find definitions for *slovenly* ("messy"), and *vulgar* ("lacking good taste"). My visual image of *floozy* based on these definitions is a woman who has a messy house with velvet Elvis pictures in each room. The sum of the parts does not equal the whole.

- The definition does not contain enough information to allow someone to use the word correctly. Imagine you have been asked to use the following words, as the dictionary defines them, in sentences:

  palatinate: the territory of a palatine
  marginalia: notes in a margin
  irremissible: not remissible
  remissible: capable of being remitted

  How helpful would those definitions be if you were truly unfamiliar with what the words mean?

Clearly, new words need to be integrated into the learner's prior knowledge, repeated in multiple contexts, and used in meaningful ways.

Planning for Integration, Repetition, and Meaningful Use

At a workshop I recently conducted in southern California, a principal told me that one of the teachers at her school was having students write the definitions of words five times because I'd said that repetition is important in teaching vocabulary. What I'd actually said in the earlier workshop was that words should be *used in a meaningful context* between ten and fifteen times. The meaningful-context aspect of my talk had completely missed the mark.

The repetition that occurs incidentally during reading has to be made explicit when teaching critical words and concepts. It takes planning, flexibility, and variety to teach vocabulary in a way that students find pleasurable and challenging. We don't want explicit word-learning strategies to take away from the joy of reading.

Baker, Simmons, and Kameenui (1995a) state that the key to increasing vocabulary development is ensuring that students with poor vocabularies not only learn the meaning of words but also have the opportunity to use them frequently. Definitions alone do not provide enough support for readers to be able to transfer those definitions to reading contexts. A social studies teacher I know spends a day a week drilling his students on the words in the glossary of their social studies textbook. When I questioned this practice, he said, "All the important stuff in the whole book is in there." I wanted to ask him why textbooks didn't just consist of glossaries then (publishing them would be a lot simpler). Instead, I told him about Nagy's (1988) research that found, "Definitions as an instructional device have substantial weaknesses and limitations that must be recognized and corrected." The ability to comprehend text entails a world of knowledge, not just the meaning of individual words. Students need to use their background knowledge to develop a deeper understanding of words and concepts.

One of the problems with word lists is that they treat all words as having equal importance in a text. Nagy (1988) points out, "Exactly what proportion of unknown words readers can tolerate depends on the nature of the text, the role of the unfamiliar words in the text, and the purpose for reading." Research studies have shown that some words can be ignored, some can be figured out in context, some will be known in relation to the reader's background knowledge, and some will be so important that they will need to be learned via conspicuous and explicit strategies. The first step is figuring out what students already know.

Assessing and Activating Related Background and Word Knowledge

Finding out what students already know about a concept and the words related to it, whether connected to a novel or a chapter in a textbook, is the first step in planning vocabulary instruction. Any of several variations on brainstorming works well to activate prior knowledge, develop multiple contexts for words, highlight relationships among words, and enlarge existing concepts. Two strategies I particularly like are list–group–label (Taba 1967) and wordstorming.

List–group–label goes like this:

1. List all the words you can think of related to _____ (major concept of text).
2. Group the words that you have listed by looking for words that have something in common.
3. Once words are grouped, decide on a label for each group.

The steps in wordstorming are:

1. Ask students to write down all the words they can think of related to a given concept, theme, or target word.
2. When students have exhausted their contributions, help them add to their individual lists by giving some specific directions:
    Can you think of words that describe someone without _____?
    Can you think of words that would show what someone might see, hear, feel, touch, smell, in a situation filled with _____?
    What are other words made from this root word?
3. Ask the students to group and label their words.
4. Introduce any words you think should be included and ask students to put them in the right group.

List–group–label was originally designed to be used in social studies classes, and it therefore works well in connection with historical fiction. If I were using the novel *The Voices of Silence* (Mooney 1997) in my social studies class, I would begin by deciding on the major concept of this book—*revolution*. Then I would ask each student to list all the words he or she could think of in connection with *revolution*. Dividing the students into groups of three or four, I would have them combine their lists of words, group them into categories, and decide on labels for these categories. (I often allow a miscellaneous category in which they can put no more than three or four words they just can't fit anywhere else.) This compilation of words then becomes our core vocabulary reference as we read the novel.

Let's take a more specific example based on the work of two students in a middle school literacy classroom. Beginning with the concept of *family*, Brittany and Crystal come up with the following lists:

Brittany's List	**Crystal's List**
dog	mom
mom	dad
sister	daughter
iguana	son
me	thankful

cousin

brother

aunt

uncle

grandma

grandpop

stepmom

niece

stepsister

stepbrother

brother-in-law

fish

bird

love

mouse

turtle

dad

stepdad

bike riding

nephew

sister-in-law

dog

bird

love

house/apartment

jobs

school

food

TV

games

shop

ice cream shop

fun

nephew

Combining their individual lists, Brittany and Crystal create the following groups and labels:

Animals	People	Activities	Family Places	Miscellaneous
dog	mom	games	jobs	food
bird	dad	shopping	house	love
cat	son	biking	apartment	thanks
iguana	daughter	fun	school	
fish	grandparents	ice cream		
turtle	stepparents	shop		
mouse	stepbrothers			
	stepsisters			

cousins

aunts

uncles

myself

As students brainstorm, they use a variety of processing skills: activating prior knowledge, identifying, listing, interpreting, categorizing, generalizing, applying, labeling. Students and teachers alike are amazed at the wealth of knowledge surrounding many concept words. Taking a word out of context and identifying multiple contexts, related words, and structural connections gives students opportunities to think outside the box. The group aspect of this activity exposes students to the thinking of others. When all the lists are pulled together, students see both what each student's thinking has in common and their commonalities as well as how it is unique.

While list–group–label works well to activate students' prior knowledge, it is also important to discuss difficult words and concepts that appear in the text. Before I read any novel with a class, I identify words I think students will need to know in order to understand the text or the theme. I copy the target words and the sentences in which they appear on an overhead transparency and give students a copy of the form in Appendix E.5. As I read each sentence aloud, I ask students to list each word in one of the four columns: "totally new," "unsure of meaning," "know one definition," or "know several ways the word can be used." (This is an abbreviated version of the strategy discussed in Chapter 2—see Appendix E.3 and E.4. It is completed individually rather than in pairs.) Words that end up in the first two columns will probably require explicit strategy lessons, although some of them may be able to be learned in context. I therefore determine which words have rich contexts (see Appendix E.2). I teach the remaining words (perhaps one a day) as part of prereading, during reading, or in postreading extensions.

The brain sorts and files new words and ideas into folders in much the same way the computer does. When I first purchased my computer, a friend asked in some astonishment, "Why do you have 128 items on your hard drive?" I had saved everything in its own space and could never find anything when I needed it. That is the very problem we eliminate for our students when we connect individual words to a broad, encompassing concept. If we create a file folder in the brain for *revolution* or *prejudice* or *oppression,* the target words can be connected to the concept. Students then learn these words in multiple contexts and in ways that allow them to use them, not just parrot them back on a test on Friday. That is meaningful learning.

Making Word Learning Meaningful

Making vocabulary study *meaningful and useful* for students has always been the difficult part. As teachers, we must help students incorporate new words into their existing language in ways that don't seem phony. A student you met in Chapter 1 was sure she would never again use the word *bourgeois.* Granted, *bourgeois* was not a common word in northern Maine. But part of the problem was the student's limited understanding of the word. When I asked why she wouldn't use the word, she responded, "If I wanted to say someone was middle class or a capitalist, I would say that, not bourgeois." When I suggested she might use the word if she wanted to chide someone who seemed overly concerned with material possessions, her response was great: "Why would I call that kind of person a capitalist? I'd call her shallow." And so it goes. Vocabulary instruction that consists of cursory memorization of words lasts just long enough to pass a test as long as the test doesn't ask students to look at multiple levels of meaning. As teachers, we must structure word learning so that it is both meaningful *and* lasting.

Each of the strategies in this chapter gives students the opportunity to integrate words into their current vocabulary and use them in a meaningful way. Some of the strategies work better for certain words and concepts than others. Any can be used in any content area, with students in grades 2 through 12. The richness of discussion surrounding any and all of them adds to the body of knowledge that students bring to their reading and writing. With this repertoire at their fingertips, teachers can choose support that best fits the word/concept being taught.

Our goals dictate our instructional methods. Given that all words in a text are not equally important, our teaching methods change in relation to our word-learning goal (see Figure 3.1). The strategy lessons that follow will most likely be used with the first and third goals: teaching content-specific words and making word-learning strategies automatic. They fall into four broad categories: building concept knowledge; activating and extending background knowledge; word analysis; and making personal and academic connections. While some lessons contain all of these elements, the lessons are grouped by the central feature. For example, while the context–content–experience graphic does ask for background knowledge, its significance is the way it helps students make personal and cross-curricular applications of a word.

Building Concept Knowledge

Concept Attainment

When I first began reading about concept mastery, I wanted to believe that individual concepts could be mastered all at once, never to be dealt with again. After several years of teaching, I realized that concepts are first only partially known; then, time, repeated exposures, and literacy maturity allow one to flesh out the concept. Lee Corey, a teacher in Orlando, Florida, used the concept attainment organizer in Appendix E.6 with a ninth-grade English class about to study the civil rights movement. Lee had the students read four short pieces related to the 1963 Sunday school bombing in Birmingham. Then they worked through the characteristics of the concept of integration based on the background

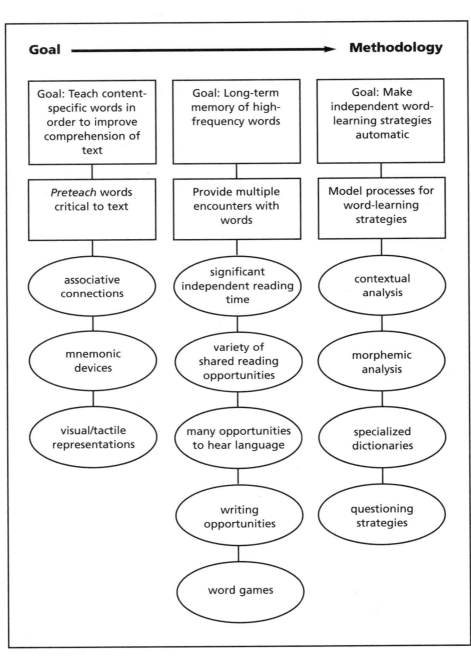

Figure 3.1

knowledge they had gained (see Figure 3.2). Asking students to refine and synthesize their understanding of a concept based on examples and nonexamples and from that forming a definition built by the entire class allows students to construct a mental file folder. Based on their reading and discussion, Lee's students determined that they would probably find people or things "mixed together/combined" and probably would not find "all white or black schools/racism" if they were witnessing integration. They then determined their class working definition for the word, "To put different things in same group/whole." As they went on to connect this word to places where they would see

Figure 3.2

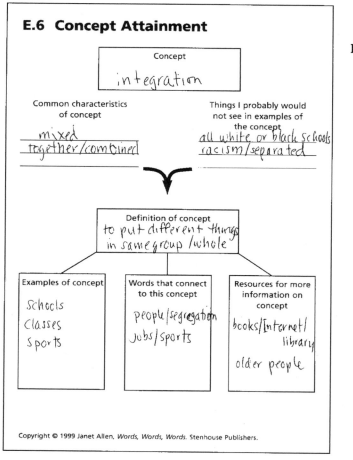

E.6 Concept Attainment

Concept

integration

Common characteristics
of concept

*mixed
together/combined*

Things I probably would
not see in examples of
the concept

*all white or black schools
racism/separated*

Definition of concept

*to put different things
in same group/whole*

Examples of concept

*Schools
Classes
Sports*

Words that connect
to this concept

*people/segregation
jobs/sports*

Resources for more
information on
concept

*books/Internet/
library
older people*

examples of this concept (schools, classes, sports), other words they know related to the concept word (people, segregation, jobs, sports), and resources for more information (books, Internet, library, and older people), they were able to identify places they might encounter this word and meaningful ways they could use this word in speaking and writing.

Concept Ladder

The concept ladder (Gillet and Temple 1982) is an excellent tool for helping students understand critical characteristics of a concept; it asks students a variety of questions related to the concept (see Appendix E.7). If a teacher is about to study rotary engines, he or she might use this device as a way to determine what students already know and what areas might still need research and teaching. What does a rotary engine look like? What was it used for? What are its parts and what is it made of? What did it replace or what has replaced it? It is a kind of _____? It might also be called a _____? As students respond to these questions as a class, the teacher categorizes and refines their responses and determines what resources will be necessary to develop a deeper knowledge of the rotary engine. The questions would change if the concept ladder is used in connection with a more abstract concept, such as prejudice: Effects of? Roots of? Related to? Caused by? Seen in? Connected to? Examples of? Eliminated by?

Making Connections by Association

This organizer (see Appendix E.8) helps students associate word relationships. The example in Figure 3.3 was completed with elementary students. After reading Chris Van Allsburg's picture book *The Polar Express,* which features a *train* and a *conductor,* students explored words that denoted similar relationships. The teacher listed other modes of transportation in the circles (plane, bus, car, ship) and for each had students determine a word that is analagous to a conductor (a bus

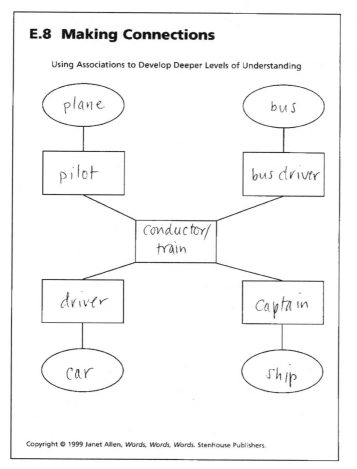

E.8 Making Connections

Using Associations to Develop Deeper Levels of Understanding

Figure 3.3

plane — pilot — conductor/train — driver — car

bus — bus driver — conductor/train — captain — ship

driver is in charge of a bus; a captain is in charge of a ship). Although this is a basic structure for associations, it is particularly helpful for new learners of English as they make connections between and among words with similar relationships.

Understanding a Concept: "ABC x 2"

The "ABC x 2" graphic (see Appendix E.9) helps students develop deep structural knowledge of words/concepts that are central to a text or unit of study. Knowledge like this is critical for students to be able to connect new information discovered in the reading back to the concept. This organizer can be started before study begins as a way of assessing and building background knowledge and then continued throughout the unit.

For example, if my students were about to begin reading *Twelve Days in August,* by Liza Ketchum Murrow, I would want to discuss the concept of personal responsibility. When I use this organizer, I always begin with the "B" column, asking students to *brainstorm* any words that come to mind. We then extend these words by *bridging* them to other areas of their lives. What does personal responsibility look like in school? In friendships? On a job? We then *analyze* the word(s) used to designate the concept. The word *response* is in *responsibility.* Is there any connection there? Does *personal* responsibility mean you're the only one involved? At this point, I ask students to "quick write" in the *apply* section about a time when they had to exhibit personal responsibility. In the "C" boxes, we then *compare* and *contrast* personal responsibility with family/community/global responsibility. What characteristics do they have in common? In what ways is personal responsibility different from the others? This process models the ways we place new information into the context of what we already know and thereby extend our knowledge.

Activating and Extending Background Knowledge
Exclusion Brainstorming

Exclusion brainstorming (Blachowicz 1986) helps students activate and build prior knowledge of a topic as a way of learning new words or phrases that connect to a larger concept. The example in Figure 3.4 was used by a high school social studies teacher who was beginning a study of factory reform in this coun-

---

Exclusion Brainstorming
(Blachowicz 1986)

factory reform

hate	investigation	rules
reparations	safety	acquittal
disaster	insurance	locked doors
fairness	floor	quiet
humanitarian	survivor	unharmed
fire	employees	

Directions: Cross out the words you don't think will be found in this selection and circle those you are likely to find.

Figure 3.4

try. The teacher chose words that appeared in the material (textbooks, resources, audiovisual aids) the students would be encountering. After talking briefly about the Triangle Shirtwaist tragedy, in which over one hundred women died in a fire in a garment factory where they worked, she asked her students to work in pairs or small groups and decide which words they expected to find in selections related to factory reform and which they didn't.

Regardless of their choices, thinking and talking about why a word might or might not appear enlarges students' thinking about language as it relates to a specific event. Students can revisit the words after they've read the material to see whether their guesses have held true. Talking about what words fit, how words they didn't anticipate made their way into the text about the topic, and ways that common words took on uncommon meanings in relation to the topic are all rich learning experiences.

Predict-O-Gram

Predict-o-gram, another Blachowicz (1986) strategy, is based on the same principle as exclusion brainstorming. Known and unknown

---

Predict-O-Gram
(Blachowicz 1986)

Directions: Predict how you think Kathryn Lasky will use these words to tell us the story of *True North*.

Boston	Afrika
shipments	Lucy Bradforth Wentworth
1858	Underground Railroad
secrets	whipping
spy	Virginia
fugitives	rumors
fugitive slave law	fortress
rich bride	"The Liberator"

Figure 3.5

words, phrases, places, and dates are combined and used to predict story plots and character relationships. In the example in Figure 3.5, I chose elements from Kathryn Lasky's novel *True North,* whose two parallel stories recount the search for freedom by two adolescent girls: one escaping slavery via the Underground Railroad and the other escaping a planned society marriage. The predict-o-gram focuses students' discussion around a narrow selection of words as they anticipate how these words will be included in the story.

Knowledge Chart

Lee Corey used a knowledge chart (see Appendix E.10) with her class of tenth graders when they were reading Lois Lowry's *The Giver.* She pulled three brief articles from the Internet, all of which discussed euthanasia. Before her students read about the "release" in *The Giver,* Lee had them list everything they knew about euthanasia. As you see in Figure 3.6, one student made it quite clear that her existing knowledge was zero. After reading the articles, this student knew the word's derivation and common meaning, as well as facts about types, legali-

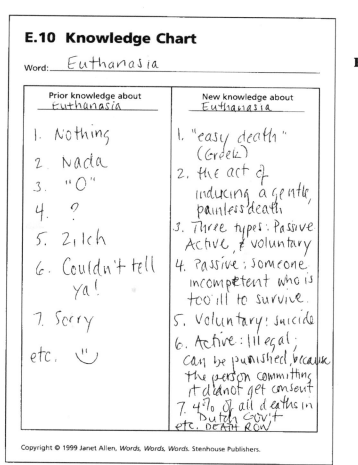

E.10 Knowledge Chart

Word: _Euthanasia_

Figure 3.6

Prior knowledge about Euthanasia	New knowledge about Euthanasia
1. Nothing	1. "easy death" (Greek)
2. Nada	2. the act of inducing a gentle, painless death
3. "0"	3. Three types: Passive Active, & voluntary
4. ?	4. Passive: someone incompetent who is too ill to survive.
5. Zilch	5. Voluntary: suicide
6. Couldn't tell ya!	6. Active: Illegal; can be punished, because the person committing it didnot get consent
7. Sorry	7. 4% of all deaths in Dutch Gov't
etc. ☺	etc. DEATH ROW

Copyright © 1999 Janet Allen, *Words, Words, Words*. Stenhouse Publishers.

ty, and public policy. She can now relate all of this historical and contemporary information to the critical moment of release in *The Giver*.

Concept and Word Analysis

Analysis Map

The analysis map in Appendix E.11 is particularly useful in social studies classes. The example in Figure 3.7 comes from Christine Landaker's Orlando, Florida, middle school

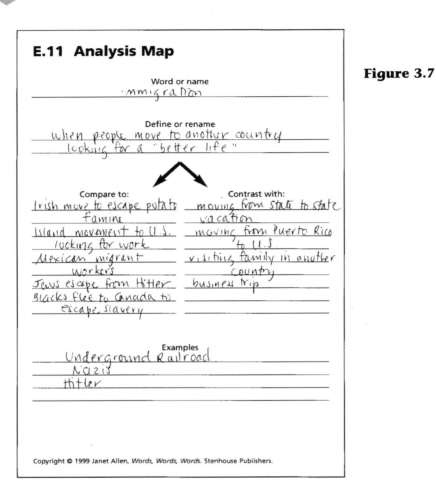

E.11 Analysis Map

Figure 3.7

Word or name

immigration

Define or rename

when people move to another country
looking for a "better life"

Compare to:

Irish move to escape potato
famine
Island movement to U.S.
looking for work
Mexican migrant
workers
Jews escape from Hitler
Blacks flee to Canada to
escape slavery

Contrast with:

moving from state to state
vacation
moving from Puerto Rico
to U.S
visiting family in another
country
business trip

Examples

Underground Railroad
Nazis
Hitler

social studies class, which is studying immigration. Christine uses this
analysis map to help students make the distinction between pleasure
or business travel and the social and economic conditions that might
force someone to relocate to a new country. The map was begun while
the class was reading their textbook and several related novels, and
will be extended as students list more names, places, and dates, in the
"examples" box. With this kind of analysis, students are able to connect historical events to contemporary events that have been similarly
motivated.

Context–Content–Experience

The context-content-experience organizer (see Appendix E.12) identifies possible definitions based on context, then zeros in on a consensus definition. The teacher prompts show how the word might be used in various content areas in school and life. Finally, students write about personal experiences associated with the word or concept. In the example in Figure 3.8, students examined the word *metamorphosis* in the context of someone's changed appearance after losing a great deal of weight. Students worked toward a definition by identifying three words that fit this context:

Figure 3.8

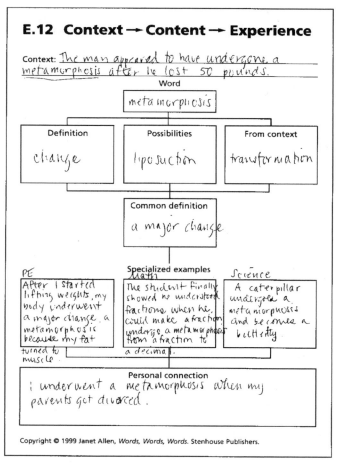

E.12 Context → Content → Experience

Context: _The man appeared to have undergone a metamorphosis after he lost 50 pounds._

Word

metamorphosis

Definition	Possibilities	From context
change	liposuction	transformation

Common definition

a major change

Specialized examples

PE

After I started lifting weights, my body underwent a major change, a metamorphosis because my fat turned to muscle.

Math

The student finally showed he understood fractions when he could make a fraction undergo a metamorphosis from a fraction to a decimal.

Science

A caterpillar undergoa a metamorphosis and becomes a butterfly.

Personal connection

i underwent a metamorphosis when my parents got divorced.

change, liposuction, and *transformation.* They eventually decided that a metamorphosis was not just a change, but a major change. In a class discussion, students brainstormed about how this word might be applied in several content areas and contexts: physical education, math, and science. Finally, the students applied the word to their own life, writing about a metamorphosis they had undergone or would like to undergo. This personal connection prompts students to consider a word in terms of how it can be used in their own speaking and writing.

Linear Arrays

Linear arrays are visual representations of degree. Appendix E.13 is a graphic organizer for depicting gradations between two related words (this one has three intervening cells, but more or fewer may be used). In the example in Figure 3.9, students created degrees of temperature, size, rank, and time.

Figure 3.9

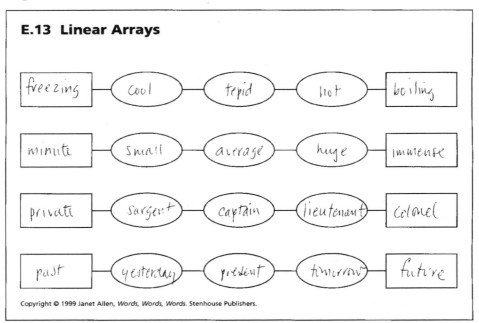

E.13 Linear Arrays

freezing — cool — tepid — hot — boiling

minute — small — average — huge — immense

private — sargent — captain — lieutenant — colonel

past — yesterday — present — tomorrow — future

Copyright © 1999 Janet Allen, *Words, Words, Words.* Stenhouse Publishers.

Barbara Barkemeyer, who teaches at Jefferson Middle School in Long Beach, California, uses a form of linear array in her English language development classes to help students examine adverbs. First she asks whether her students know what *never* means and elicits examples of how *never* is used in everyday speech. Then she does the same with *always*. Next she writes *always* at the top of a sheet of paper, *never* at the bottom, and asks the students to generate a list of adverbs that would fall somewhere in between. Finally, she writes each of the students' suggestions on a separate card and has her students arrange the cards in descending order (see below):

always
certain
frequently
often
likely
probably
more than even
even chance
less than even
occasionally
unlikely
seldom
rarely
never

An activity like this helps students examine subtle distinctions in words.

Part to Whole

The part-to-whole organizer (see Appendix E.14) gives students the opportunity to explore prefixes, root words, and suffixes by repeating the common word part. The example in Figure 3.10 was used in conjunction with a dognapping story in which the dog is *unleashed*.

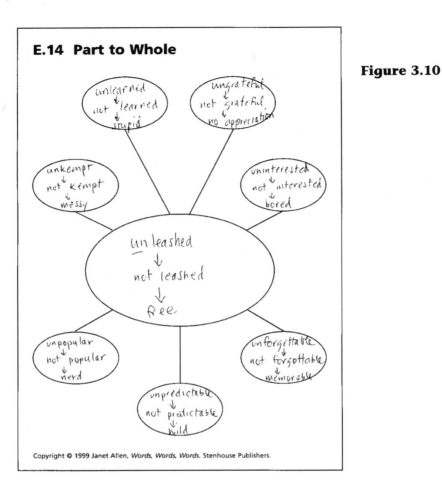

E.14 Part to Whole

Figure 3.10

- unlearned → not learned → stupid
- ungrateful → not grateful → no appreciation
- unkempt → not kempt → messy
- uninterested → not interested → bored
- unleashed → not leashed → free
- unpopular → not popular → nerd
- unforgettable → not forgettable → memorable
- unpredictable → not predictable → wild

Students easily figure this word out from the context, and the teacher then leads them to look at other words where *un* also means not, introducing words of increasing difficulty. In this case, students generated *ungrateful, uninterested, unforgettable, unpredictable,* and *unpopular.* The teacher suggested *unkempt* and *unlearned.* Each time a new *un* word is inserted, the *not* pattern is repeated so students learn that the prefix *un* is predictable. Then a synonym that is already part of the students' vocabulary is arrived at. For example: the students move from *unkempt* to a direct structural analysis (*un* means *not, not kempt* [kept]), to a definition (not clean or organized, or *messy*).

Words in Context

In the first words-in-context organizer (see Appendix E.15), students have the opportunity to try to figure out the meaning of a word using a combination of word parts and context. In the example in Figure 3.11, students take apart the word *unpredictable* by examining what the prefix *un* and the root word *predict* mean. They then test their knowledge of the word parts by listing other words that have either the same prefix or the same root. Finally, the students write their own definition of the word in the context of the sentence based on their knowl-

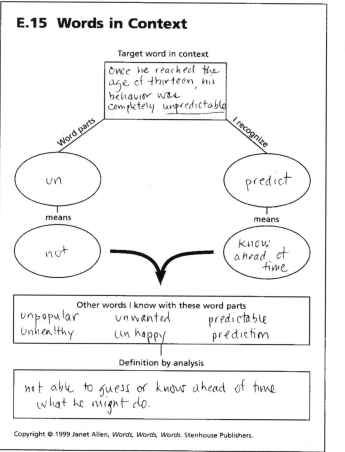

Figure 3.11

E.15 Words in Context

Target word in context

> Once he reached the age of thirteen, his behavior was completely unpredictable

Word parts

I recognize

un

predict

means

means

not

know ahead of time

Other words I know with these word parts

unpopular	unwanted	predictable
Unhealthy	un happy	prediction

Definition by analysis

> not able to guess or know ahead of time what he might do.

edge of the prefix and root-word meanings. The study of prefixes, suffixes, and root words can be extended as an ongoing part of the curriculum by asking students to develop word lists using their knowledge
of word parts (see Appendix D for examples).

For words requiring in-depth study, a second words-in-context
organizer (see Appendix E.16) gives students concrete synonyms and
antonyms on which to anchor the word. (I adapted this organizer from
one I saw Adams and Cerqui [1989] use at a reading styles workshop.)
The sentence that contains the unknown or unfamiliar word is written
at the top of the transparency, and the target word is put in the center
box. In the box above, students enter a working definition of the word
based on context clues and structural analysis. (If students are unable
to generate this definition, I send them to the dictionary or give them
a definition with an example.) In the three boxes on the right, students
list synonyms for the word. In the three ovals on the left, they list
antonyms. In the boxes and ovals at the bottom, the meaning of the
words is personalized in a concrete, memorable way. In the example in
Figure 3.12 I asked my students to give me examples of a basketball
player whose appearance would and would not be considered preposterous by some people, examples of something in the animal kingdom
whose appearance is and isn't unbelievable or bizarre, and examples
of something that a middle school student might say that a teacher
would and would not consider unexpected. (The prompt you create is
critical, because you want to elicit striking examples.)

This organizer should first be used with the whole class; after that,
it can be completed by smaller groups. However, it is not an individual
activity. One of my graduate students once asked me for some ways to
teach vocabulary. I gave her this form, and she and other members of
her English department began using it in their classes. A few weeks
later, she confessed that her students were really bored with the activity. I asked her how she was conducting it. "Well," she said, "we ran
three thousand copies of the form and asked students to find five words
they didn't know in their independent reading. They then had to com-

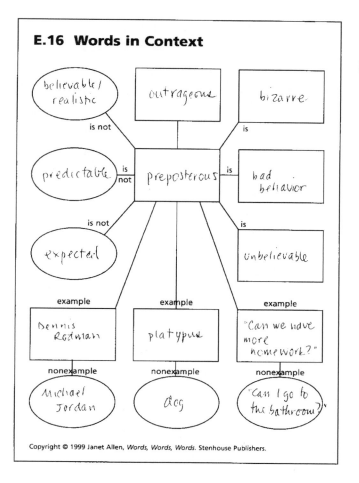

E.16 Words in Context

Figure 3.12

plete one of these forms for each of the words." This is definitely not the way to go! If you truly don't know a word, it is virtually impossible to complete this form. If you do know the word well enough to complete the form, you don't need to complete it. Students learn extended meanings of the target word here by virtue of their *joint* knowledge.

Word Questioning

Teachers are often asked to demonstrate that they are moving students to higher and more critical levels of understanding. The graphic organizer in Appendix E.17 prompts students to ask questions at several levels of thinking: analysis, comprehension, application, analysis, synthesis, knowledge, and evaluation. The example in Figure 3.13 was generated by fifth graders who were about to read a story about students who visit some cave dwellings on their class trip. The teacher read the target word in context ("The class trip they took to the cave dwellings made the students feel like *archeologists*"), and the students considered the model questions, starting with the analysis cell and working clockwise.

Each level of thinking in this organizer increases students' understanding of the target word. Over time, students should begin to inter-

Figure 3.13

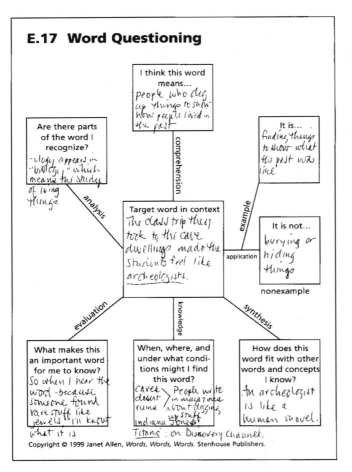

nalize these questions that will help them discover and extend the meanings of words.

Making Personal and Academic Connections

Making Associations

Figure 3.14 was generated by a group of high school students who were reading *Fair Game,* a novel by Erika Tamar. In the novel, several members of a football team have raped a

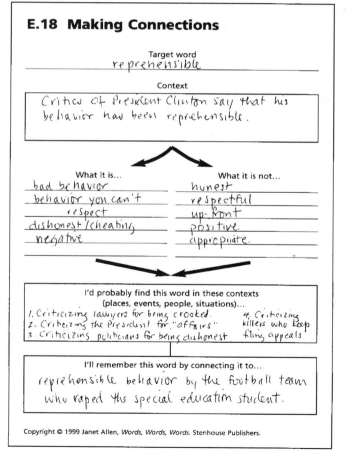

Figure 3.14

E.18 Making Connections

Target word
reprehensible

Context
Critics of President Clinton say that his behavior has been reprehensible.

What it is...
bad behavior
behavior you can't respect
dishonest/cheating
negative

What it is not...
honest
respectful
up-front
positive
appropriate

I'd probably find this word in these contexts (places, events, people, situations)...
1. Criticizing lawyers for being crooked.
2. Criticizing the President for "affairs"
3. Criticizing politicians for being dishonest
4. Criticizing killers who keep filing appeals.

I'll remember this word by connecting it to...
reprehensible behavior by the football team who raped the special education student.

special education student in their high school, and the administrators don't report the incident until after the season's playoffs. Students began by exploring the term *reprehensible* in connection with behavior currently being discussed on the news or in magazines and newspapers; it was no surprise when they came up with President Clinton's. Students then integrated the term into their lives by giving examples of things people might do that they would and would not find reprehensible. Students then brainstormed examples of contexts (places, events, people, situations) where reprehensible behavior would be witnessed. Finally, they connected their analysis to the behavior of the characters in the novel. (A blank version of this form is included in Appendix E.18.)

Multiple Meanings

Multiple meanings of words can be explored using Appendix E.19. In the example in Figure 3.15, the target word in context (*disdainfully*) is taken from Bel Mooney's *The Voices of Silence*. Students first look at general times/events when one might treat someone with disdain. Then they record specific times when they, or others, have treated someone or something with a disdainful attitude. Moving from the general to the specific allows students to begin to own the word in their lives. As teachers and students talk through each of these examples, students take note of "family" words and develop a deeper understanding of how the prefixes and suffixes of words change depending on how the word is used in the sentence.

Sensory Language Chart

The sensory language chart (Appendix E.20) is particularly helpful for students who have difficulty getting the impact of a story, poem, or historical event because they have difficulty visualizing the situation or empathizing with the characters. In the example in Figure 3.16, middle school students have cited words or phrases (both at the beginning of the story and at the end) that set the mood in Ramsey Campbell's

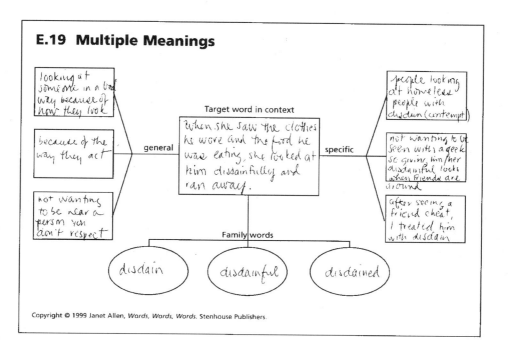

E.19 Multiple Meanings

looking at someone in a bad way because of how they look

because of the way they act

not wanting to be near a person you don't respect

general

Target word in context

When she saw the clothes he wore and the food he was eating, she looked at him disdainfully and ran away.

specific

people looking at homeless people with disdain (contempt)

not wanting to be seen with a geek so giving him/her disdainful looks when friends are around

after seeing a friend cheat, I treated him with disdain

Family words

disdain   disdainful   disdained

Copyright © 1999 Janet Allen, *Words, Words, Words.* Stenhouse Publishers.

Figure 3.15

"Heading Home." In each case, I asked students to close their eyes and imagine they were the main character who was "heading home" (in this case, literally using his head and only his head in order to climb some stairs). What do you see? What do you hear in the room above you? What do you smell? What do you taste as you use your jaw to move? What do you touch? This activity helps students learn to choose words carefully depending on audience and purpose, both in their speaking and in their writing. They see how changing one word can change the entire tone or context.

Thinking Trees

I adapted "thinking trees" (see Appendix E.21) from Kirby and Kuykendall's work (1991). This graphic works particularly well with concepts appropriate for group research. In the example in Figure 3.17, the concept up for discussion is *communicable diseases*. Students

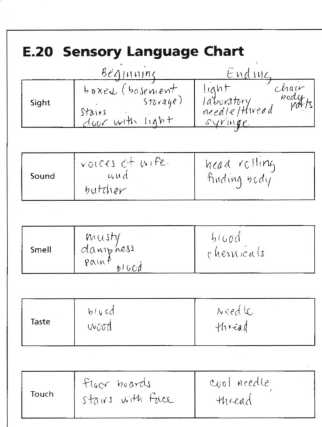

E.20 Sensory Language Chart

Figure 3.16

	Beginning	Ending
Sight	boxes (basement storage) Stairs door with light	light chair laboratory body needle/thread parts syringe
Sound	voices of wife and butcher	head rolling finding body
Smell	musty dampness paint blood	blood chemicals
Taste	blood wood	Needle thread
Touch	floor boards stairs with face	cool needle thread

suggest several communicable diseases they know, beginning, of course, with AIDS. Then, in groups, they research causes for each communicable disease and list solutions that might be tried.

Understanding Characters Through Character Traits

Teachers who ask their students to analyze characters are often dismayed by responses like "He was cute" or "She was a duh." Hardly the stuff of critical analysis! Part of the reason for these responses has to do with how few words students actually know that would describe a character and his or her motivations. They need to be helped to explore

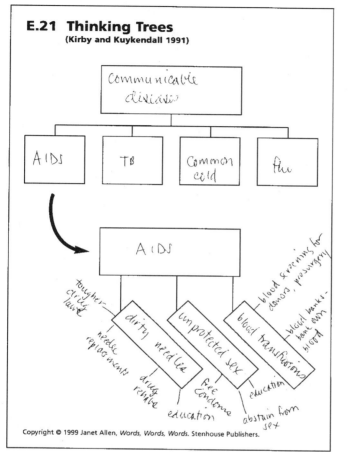

E.21 Thinking Trees
(Kirby and Kuykendall 1991)

Figure 3.17

language that describes and define characters. The graphic organizer in Figure 3.18, which I use in connection with John Christopher's *The White Mountains,* is a simple example. On the left side of the page, I list words that might be used to describe the characters, who are listed horizontally across the page. After we spend time defining the words through context, example, or explicit instruction, we begin reading the novel. Every day or two, we check to see which characters are exhibiting which traits. Did we see any examples of so-and-so being abrupt? imaginative? prudent? If we did, we check off that characteristic for that character. When the novel is finished, students can take this sheet of character traits and use it as a prewriting organizer.

Understand the Characters Through Looking at Character Traits

Title: *The White Mountains*

	Jack	"Beanpole"	Will	Henry	Eloise
abrupt					
easygoing					
understanding					
entertaining					
harsh					
placid					
stern					
quarrelsome					
imaginative					
selfish					
pessimistic					
optimistic					
noble					
prudent					
selfless					
honest					
independent					

Figure 3.18

Gail Sherman's middle school students at Glenridge Middle School used this strategy to look at the characteristics of the main characters in S. E. Hinton's *The Outsiders* (see Figure 3.19). When you use this organizer, remember that not all students will attribute the same characteristics to each of the characters.

Word in My Context

This graphic organizer gives students the opportunity to illustrate the meaning of a word in the context of their own lives. The dictionary is the initial resource, and the definitions it offers are discussed. Students then generate good and bad connections with the word and illustrate their understanding of the word by drawing something from their life that represents the word. This visual, along with writing in which the

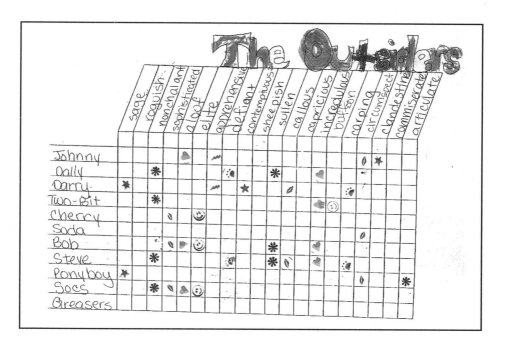

Figure 3.19

students use the word in an anecdote from their own life, makes the word and its definitions come alive. This organizer is particularly useful for middle school students who enjoy drawing. In the example in Figure 3.20, one of Robin Miller-Jenkins's middle school students in Orlando connects the word *miserable* to an event in her life. It sounds as though this young woman might have the opportunity to use this word again many times!

McKeown et al. (1985) argue, "Many encounters with a new word are necessary if vocabulary instruction is to have a measurable effect on reading comprehension." The strategies discussed in this chapter offer students multiple opportunities to see a word in new contexts, to connect a word with related knowledge they may already possess, and to integrate a word into their own reading and writing experiences. Nagy (1988) contends, "Methods of vocabulary instruction that most effectively improve comprehension of text containing the instructed word go far beyond providing definitions and contexts." Students are more

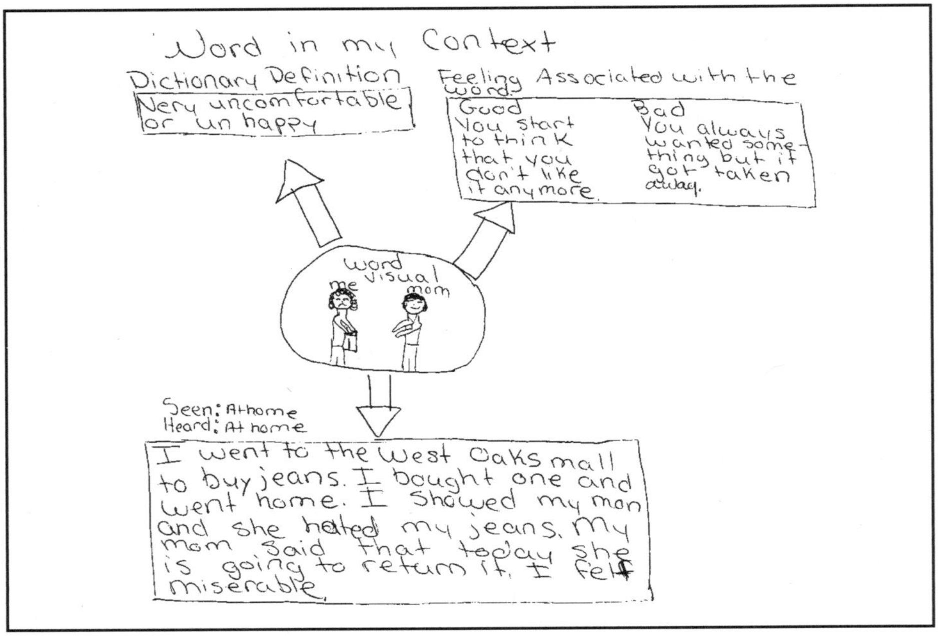

Figure 3.20

likely to use words they have recorded and worked with in organizers like those discussed here. With each use, the chances increase that they will continue to use these words in speaking and writing and recognize them in their reading.

Unfortunately, we can't teach hundreds of words at this same level of intensity. Fortunately, we don't need to. Classrooms rich in reading, writing, talk, and language play present multiple opportunities to learn new words. These strategies, thoughtfully chosen, should be reserved for words that are critical to a concept being studied. Robert Frost was quoted as saying that there are two kinds of teachers: those who fill you with so much quail shot that you can't move and those that give you a prod and you jump to the skies. Balance is as critical in a vocabulary program as it is in everything else we do in literacy education. We wouldn't want our students to get so weighted down with the quail shot of vocabulary organizers that they can't pick up the books in which the words are used.

Reading as the Heart of Word-Rich Classrooms

Polonius: What do you read, my lord?
Hamlet: Words, words, words.

William Shakespeare, *Hamlet*

I was pleasantly surprised to receive a recent issue of *Time* magazine whose cover touted the article, "How to Make Your Kid a Better Student." I was even more pleased when I read the article and found reading strongly advocated as making better students *and* helping them achieve higher SAT scores. The article reports that Tom Parker, director of admissions at Williams College, in Massachusetts, believes reading to be the key (Wallis 1998, 83). When parents ask what they should do to increase their children's SAT scores, he tells them to make sure their children read. "The best SAT-preparation course in the world is to read to your children in bed when they're little. Eventually, if that's a wonderful experience for them, they'll start to read for themselves." The article continues, "Parker says he has never met a kid with high scores on the verbal section of the SAT who wasn't a passionate reader." Parker's comment underscores the research that has supported reading as a critical ingredient in learning new words. Fielding, Wilson, and Anderson (1986) find that the amount of free-choice reading is the best predictor of vocabulary growth between grades 2 and 5. Further, Nagy (1988) states, "What is needed to produce vocabulary growth is not more vocabulary instruction, but more reading." Baker,

Simmons, and Kameenui (1995a) cite Anderson and Nagy's (1991) and Baumann and Kameenui's (1991) research as a basis for this statement about the significance of reading: "However, reading is probably the most important mechanism for vocabulary growth throughout a student's school-age years and beyond." When I share this research with teachers, their next question is, So, what would that look like in a classroom? Let's look at some possibilities.

Vocabulary to, with, and by

Mooney's book *Reading to, with and by Children* (1990) talks about the approaches to reading found in balanced literacy classrooms. In "to" reading, the teacher reads to the students in a way that communicates the "charm, magic, impact and appeal" of language. "With" reading encompasses both shared and guided reading. During shared reading, the teacher or another fluent reader (e.g., the reader on a recording, an instructional aide, a parent/community volunteer) reads the text while the students follow along in individual copies of the text. In guided reading, students decode text while the teacher serves as a strategic guide. Shared reading and guided reading offer teachers multiple and diverse opportunities to teach new words and word-learning strategies; word learning can be brought to a conscious level in the following ways:

- Use context to figure out meanings.
- Demonstrate how to use dictionaries, thesauruses, and handbooks as resources.
- Highlight the importance of specialized vocabulary.
- Connect individual words to a larger concept.
- Show why some words require deeper understanding than other words.
- Create visuals, webs, or organizers to develop memory links for words.
- Extend knowledge by pointing out multiple meanings.

- Show students how you learn incidental words.
- Help students discriminate between common knowledge and specialized vocabulary.

In "by" reading, students have the option (each day in elementary school and several times a week in secondary school) to select texts to read independently for sustained periods of time.

This chapter focuses on these three avenues for using literature and language in whole-group, small-group, paired, and individual activities. This balanced method of encountering and learning new words allows learners to experience the three critical components of vocabulary acquisition: integration, repetition, and meaningful use. Caine and Caine, in their book *Making Connections: Teaching and the Human Brain* (1994, 131), cite the importance of talk: "As we talk about a subject or skill in complex and appropriate ways—and that includes making jokes and playing games—we actually begin to feel better about the subject and master it. That is why the everyday use of relevant terms and the appropriate use of language should be incorporated in every course from the beginning."

Having Fun with Language

Words should be enjoyed, and the study of words should bring no less joy. Some of my fondest elementary school memories are of when it was too stormy to go outside and we stayed in to play hangman. I always kept commercial word games in my high school classroom (see Appendix C for a partial list)—Boggle, Scrabble, and Pictionary filled many before- and after-school student hours, and our reward days after weeks of hard work were often centered around these games. There were word games loaded onto the hard drives of each of the computers in my room, and students rushed in each morning to play those games and stayed until I forced them to leave for class. The question for many of us is, How can we replicate that excitement, and that active learning, in our more structured vocabulary time?

Word Walls

Word walls are absolutely essential in our classrooms. As teachers and students work through texts together in shared and guided reading, when students encounter familiar words but unfamiliar spellings, and when we build concept-related words or topical categories, we need to have the words in full view so that the students can see them and use them in their writing. In *The Word Wall: Teaching Vocabulary Through Immersion,* Green states a primary asset of using a word wall: "The Word Wall is built upon the spiral theory of mastery—repetition reinforces previously learned principles. Regular use throughout the school year allows you to recycle many words." When I began using word walls in my classroom, I found that so many words in a random order made students hesitant; some students were unable to access the words and use them in writing and speaking. Green's word walls each had a different background color and a different goal (e.g., phonic patterns, spelling patterns). I had more success with alphabetic and thematic word walls, which were easy to maintain, timely, easily accessible, and organized.

Word walls don't need to be complicated. Cut out the letters of the alphabet; cut some strips of construction paper and keep them handy for writing words; and get those words on the wall! Three days after starting a word wall in my classroom, I began seeing the words in students' writing. Words from the word wall sometimes made it into our graphic organizers for more study. We played a game using the words on the wall: my students stood in front of the word wall and I tossed a Nerf ball to a student, creating a word-hunt task at the same time. ("Find three words that have to do with colors," "Find two words you could use to describe how you might feel if you had just made the winning basket at the basketball game"). When that student found the words, he threw the ball to someone else and gave that person a task ("Find two action words," "Find three words that describe your date"). Their word-hunt tasks were always more interesting and risky than mine. Searching, categorizing, using words in multiple contexts, and connecting the words to their own lives were great ways to keep students aware of the words on the wall.

We also kept one area for topical/thematic words. For example, when we read Wiesner's wordless picture book *Tuesday,* we created a list of military terms gleaned from the illustrations (*camouflage, in formation, bringing in reinforcements, parachute, retreat,* etc.). Shared reading of Sweeney's *The Tiger Orchard* resulted in a list of art terms; Bloor's *Tangerine* inspired environmental terms. A class discussion about conflict resolution and problem solving prompted a list of terms related to safe discussions. An extended writing lesson on creating effective leads produced "Words That Grab You." Watching *Cry in the Wild* (the movie version of Paulsen's *Hatchet*) led to a list of survival terms, tools, and techniques. Topical lists will change frequently depending on what the class is reading, writing, and discussing. Keeper words from each list can be moved to the alphabetic word wall.

If your classroom doesn't have much wall space, you have to be more creative. Last year I was in an elementary school in California where one class was temporarily meeting in a computer room. The computers blocked the walls, and the teacher asked me where she could put her word wall. I suggested taping the construction-strip words to the plastic computer covers. There were thirty computers in the room—ample "wall" space for lots of words.

Reading the World

n *Literacy: Reading the Word and the World* (1987), Freire and Macedo discuss "reading the world" as a critical component of the act of reading: "Reading does not consist merely of decoding the written word or language; rather it is preceded by and intertwined with knowledge of the world" (29). Talented teachers all over this country know that one of the ways to make word learning meaningful and integrated is to help students make connections between the language they use and the things they read in school and the examples of language they encounter in their larger world. Teachers of language could construct lessons every day just using the newspaper (Newspapers in Education workshops conducted by local newspapers all over this country show teachers how to do just that). By comparing and contrasting the language used by two different sitcom characters or discussing an article about the derivation of the word *impeachment* (from the Latin word *impedicare,* which means tying one's feet together), students are able to see language being used in meaningful ways.

Reading the world for examples of language brings the study of words alive. Here are two more examples of what "reading the world" looks like in the classroom.

In *There's Room for Me Here* (Allen and Gonzalez 1998) Kyle Gonzalez tells about using a "word jar" (inspired by Monalisa DeGross's book *Donovan's Word Jar*) as a way to get her middle school students to pay attention to the words they read, saw, or heard. On slips of paper, students wrote down words, indicated where they had heard/read/seen the words, and said what they thought the words meant. These slips of paper were then stuffed into a huge pickle jar Kyle got from the cafeteria. Each day, Kyle pulled a word or two from the jar and the class talked about them. Appendix E.22 is a graphic representation of what the character Donovan did in DeGross's book, which was to collect words in each category and then give them to people who needed them. This organizer is a great way to help students become aware of words and their impact. Students can interview people and get their suggestions for words in each of the categories. They can add to them during shared and independent reading. Some of the words can be placed in the class word jar or on the word wall.

In his developmental writing courses at a community college, Rick Adams has his students "reading the world" at a more sophisticated level. Here's the organizational structure he stipulates for his students' journals:

1. **Homework and Notes**
   Homework Assignments
   Class/Lecture Notes
2. **In-Class and Journal Writing**
   In-Class Writing
   Journal Assignments
   Quick Write Exercises
   Study Questions from Readings
3. **Reflections**
   Thinking About the Things We're Learning in Class
4. **Quips, Clips, and Snips**
   Comics-Phrases-Issues Showing Class Ideas Occurring in the Real World
   Scrapbook and Comments on Language-Culture

The final category, "Quips, Clips, and Snips," invites students to read their world for examples of the specialized language they are using in their writing classes. Here are a few examples of what Rick's students have included in this section:

- One student copied a "Non Sequitur" cartoon (Wiley) in which a patient asks how long he will be in post-op. The doctor replies by asking the patient if he thinks the line "The way to a man's heart" is just a metaphor.
- Another student collected quotes she found related to change (JFK's "Change is the law of life" and Heraclitus's "There is nothing permanent except change") as examples of her thesis statement for her first essay.
- After a class discussion of the language and format of an argumentation essay by George Will (*Newsweek,* March 30, 1998), a student included a "Dennis the Menace" cartoon and a "Non Sequitur" cartoon showing the language of argumentation in action.

Building on the Language Students Bring

Margaret Meek, in *How Texts Teach What Readers Learn* (1988), discusses the importance of valuing what children already bring to the reading of a text. "If there is no place or chance for beginners to demonstrate what they can do, what they know will never be part of their teachers' awareness" (7). This applies to the processes of reading that children bring as well as to their acquired knowledge of words and how language works. With students who have limited knowledge of English or who have difficulty acquiring more sophisticated uses of language, reading the illustrations and generating text based on those illustrations works extremely well.

For instance, I might use an illustration from *My Freedom Trip: A Child's Escape from North Korea,* written by Frances and Ginger Park and illustrated by Debra Reid Jenkins. The story is based on the experiences of Frances and Ginger's mother; it describes—with words, Korean symbols, and oil paintings—the hazardous journey the mother took as a young child from North to South Korea prior to the Korean War. The sombre oil paintings echo the dangerous nighttime journey.

In one particular illustration young Soo and Mr. Han, her guide, have just "slipped away from the train and into the night. Up the mountain we walked, with the cries of wild animals in our ears and the moon in our eyes. The woods were all around us. Every few moments, Mr. Han would stop and listen for footsteps." Before students read the text, they can "read" this illustration through a form of guided reading prompted by questions like this:

- Tell me what you notice as you read this illustration. Take two minutes to study the illustration and list as many words as you can based on what you see here.
- What can you tell about how Soo and her guide are feeling based on their body language and facial expressions?
- The moon tells us that this is nighttime. What inference can you make based on the knowledge that Soo and her guide are traveling at night?

- Is there any indication whether this is a difficult trip or an easy trip? What are some words that we could predict the author might use to describe this journey?

- Soo and her guide are stopped. What do they appear to be doing? What words come to mind for their behavior?

- Can you make any predictions about what will happen next based on what we see here?

- Now let's look at the Korean symbol that is on the opposite page. This is the symbol for listen. How does that fit with anything that we read in the illustration?

- Let's take our word lists and our prediction lists and look at the text that accompanies this illustration. I'm going to read the words to you. Just listen to the story and then we'll read it again to see if there were words and actions that we were able to predict.

Reading the illustrations, generating words as well as story, making predictions, and confirming or rejecting those predictions all mirror the work of fluent readers. Emerging readers see their language valued as they find their words mirrored in the text. This activity can be done with a whole group using a Big Book, a transparency or color photocopy, or multiple copies of a single text.

Another way to emphasize and appreciate the language that learners bring is by creating slang dictionaries. Carl Sandburg said, "Slang is language that rolls up its sleeves, spits on its hands and gets to work." For many of our students, the language we attempt to teach them in schools doesn't "get to work" for them very effectively. Classrooms and schools have become battlegrounds for decisions about what words will be used as part of school language. For years we have discussed and debated "standard English." (Just recently, I was informed that the politically correct term is now "the language of the international marketplace.") As these debates continue, teachers struggle to teach a language that is almost nonexistent in the lives of some of their students while students create and use language they believe is more effective. I once heard a linguist say that English teachers have one of the toughest jobs around: because of the changing nature of language and usage, they are trying to teach a language that, in part, no longer exists.

One of my university students who was interning at a local urban high school was having great difficulty getting her students to use the standard English required of them in her supervising teacher's English class. My suggestion that she have students write a dictionary of the language they used and then translate that dictionary for those who didn't understand them met with immediate success. Students were diligent in collecting words, writing definitions, and using them in sentences (see Figure 4.1). They argued over the "exact definition" for terms like *git* and whether the word was a noun or a verb. Asking students to translate their dictionary into standard English "for others to use" helped them understand how language changes depending on audience and purpose. It was also effective in helping students learn that they had a range of options for designating everything from meetings with the principal to insults swapped in the parking lot. An excellent resource for a similar activity in secondary English classes is *William's Wit Kit:* these magnetic strips use Shakespeare's words and can be used to create over ten thousand insults. A print resource for this activity is Hill and Ottchen's *Shakespeare's Insults: Educating Your Wit.*

Creating Language

Children have always loved to create language, and they create it for the same reason anyone creates language—to communicate in unique ways. Usually, however, the language they create limits communication to those in the club. I'm guessing many of us remember with pleasure the day we finally learned pig latin and only those kids who knew the language could understand what we were saying. Perhaps as adults we continue to do the same. Imagine one who isn't part of the school setting dropping

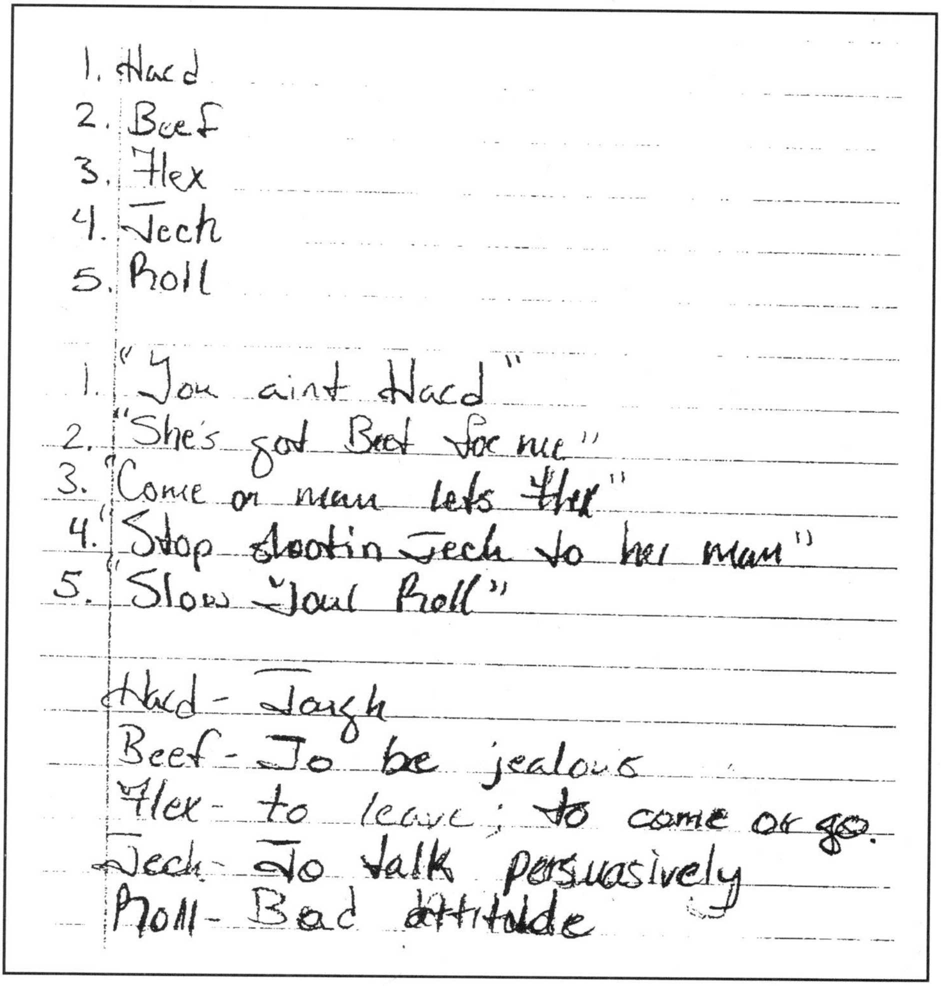

1. Hacd
2. Beef
3. Flex
4. Jech
5. Roll

1. "You aint Hacd"
2. "She's got Beef for me"
3. "Come on man lets flex"
4. "Stop shootin Jech to her man"
5. "Slow Your Roll"

Hacd - Tough
Beef - To be jealous
Flex - to leave; to come or go.
Jech - To talk persuasively
Roll - Bad attitude

Figure 4.1

into a faculty meeting and listening to a conversation centered around words and abbreviated language such as LEP, GATE, SLD, and ADHD. All specialized language has its club members, and fostering the creation of language with students in our classes helps them understand the changing and capricious nature of language. First, however, children must understand how words work.

Margaret Hill, in her chapter "Reaching Struggling Readers," in *Into Focus: Understanding and Creating Middle School Readers* (Beers and Samuels 1998), discusses multiple ways to help students understand how words are created. Structural analysis and decoding research has shown the importance of word-part knowledge, and Hill recommends several strategies for achieving it (e.g., vocabulary trees and morphology journals). Prefixes, suffixes, and roots can be studied as part of understanding a single word or as part of understanding how the same word parts are used in other words. Taking a word the students know and then constructing a list of words that can be learned using what is known about parts of the initial word is an excellent way to teach students to use what they already know as part of word attack. Students can also use the word parts listed in Appendix D to create unknown or nonsense words; other groups of students can then figure out the meaning of these words based on their word-part knowledge.

There are many classroom activities teachers can use to help students understand how a language system is created, but I'll highlight here some activities and resources my students have particularly enjoyed. The first comes from Christenbury and Kelly's *Questioning: A Path to Critical Thinking* (1983, 32). In this code-breaking activity, shapes represent parts of speech (e.g., a circle = an article; a square = a noun; etc.). Students are given several shape "sentences" (e.g., circle, square, triangle, heart, circle, diamond, square) that follow the code the teacher has created. To break the code, students must use their knowledge of the way sentences and words work. Then they create their own sentence in which the words match the function represented by the shapes.

Alvin Schwartz's *Kickle Snifters and other Fearsome Critters Collected from American Folklore* (1976) is an excellent resource for strengthening students' creativity with identification and description. Schwartz has collected the names of a variety of creatures from American folklore. Descriptions and illustrations for creatures such as the snawfus, squonk, lufferlang, glyptodont, and squidgicum-squee inspire students to create their own encyclopedias of unusual creatures.

Ed Young (1997) has created an exquisite picture book that explores twenty-six Chinese characters. Each character describes a feeling or emotion, and each illustration contains the symbol for heart. The illustrations and characters explore concepts such as shame (the heart knows right from wrong), virtue (the heart is good), and despair (an anxious heart). As students study the Chinese characters, they can create other concept words based on ways they connect individual characters.

When the poet and anthologist Paul Janeczko visited our high school classes, my students were intrigued with Paul the poet and Paul the person. I purchased all of his books for our classroom and students spent many hours reading the poetry and adding his poems to the individual poetry anthologies they created. The book that received the most attention, however, was not one of his poetry collections but *Loads of Codes and Secret Ciphers* (1994). The book is filled with basic code and cipher systems, and includes exercises asking readers to break codes, translate sentences from pig latin and turkey Irish into English, and create their own codes. (Unfortunately, the code-creating activities worked so well, I was the one left outside the "club." I had to delve into *Loads of Codes* carefully before I could read their papers!)

A World War II picture book, *The Unbreakable Code,* written by Sara Hoagland Hunter and illustrated by Julia Miner, is an excellent resource for showing students the historical importance of code. This book tells the story of Navajo code talkers, who passed more than eight hundred messages in two days during the invasion of Iwo Jima. The Japanese never could break the code. It is a story rich in cultural pride and symbolic language.

Preparing for the SAT

With the new SAT placing an even greater emphasis on reading, my advice is obvious: increase the time, amount, and variety of reading children experience.

An associate of mine, a co-owner of a book recording company, and his teenage daughter panicked during the months before the daughter was to take her SAT. He complained that her teachers weren't giving her any SAT lists. Her PSAT scores had been low, and she was doing almost no reading. My advice? "Get her reading. Ignore lists. You own thousands of books on tape; make sure she's listening to them." Sure enough, after six months of intense reading, she was hooked as a reader and her test scores increased considerably.

For most teachers, parents, and school administrators, however, that advice just isn't enough. So, *in addition to* (not instead of) rich reading experiences, I offer here three commercial resources that some teachers say have helped them prepare students for the SAT. The first resource is a novel, *Tooth and Nail: A Novel Approach to the New SAT,* by Charles Elster and Joseph Elliot (1994). The novel highlights words that have a "better-than-average chance of appearing on the SAT." In order to create the novel, Elster and Elliot "analyzed the verbal sections of thirty-five published SATs administered from 1980 to 1990 and all the preview materials available for SAT I." They then pared the list down to the most challenging words, all of which they used in the novel. These words are presented in boldface and are defined in the glossary. In addition, there are several pages of test-preparation exercises at the end of the novel. When I read the novel, the boldfaced words distracted me from the story, but I learned some new words. (Jill Perry, a high school calculus teacher, told me that some of her students had this same mixed reaction.) Nothing works for everyone, but at least this resource is based on reading.

Last year at IRA, I discovered two books by Sam, Max, and Bryan Burchers: *Vocabutoons* (1997) and *Vocabutoons: Elementary Edition* (1998). These cartoons are humorous, visual mnemonics (a mnemonic helps you remember something by associating it with something you already know). The authors state, "The words selected as Vocabutoons are those frequently found in the S.A.T. and G.R.E." Each page contains a target word, its phonetic pronunciation, the definition, a mnemonic link, a cartoon, and one or more sentences that link the target word to the cartoon. An example is shown in Figure 4.2. The link here is the sound of the word: *mores* sounds like *more A's*. The cartoon contrasts a child being applauded for lots of A's with a child, in a dunce cap, relegated to a stool in the corner. Teachers use the books in a variety of ways. An elementary teacher in south Florida uses a page a day; students discuss the word and brainstorm other links, cartoons, and sentences. A high school teacher told me that her students apply the

Figure 4.2

MORES (MAWR ayz)
Customary cultural standards; moral attitudes, manners, habits
Link: More A's

"Our educational MORES have it that the MORE A's a student makes, the better their education."

- According to Chinese MORES, it is considered polite for dinner guests to belch at the table as a gesture of appreciation and enjoyment.
- It is said that a certain actress of her acquaintance has dubious morals and disregards the accepted MORES for married women.
- The problem with some community MORES is that the older generation clings to outdated moral attitudes no longer appropriate for the times.

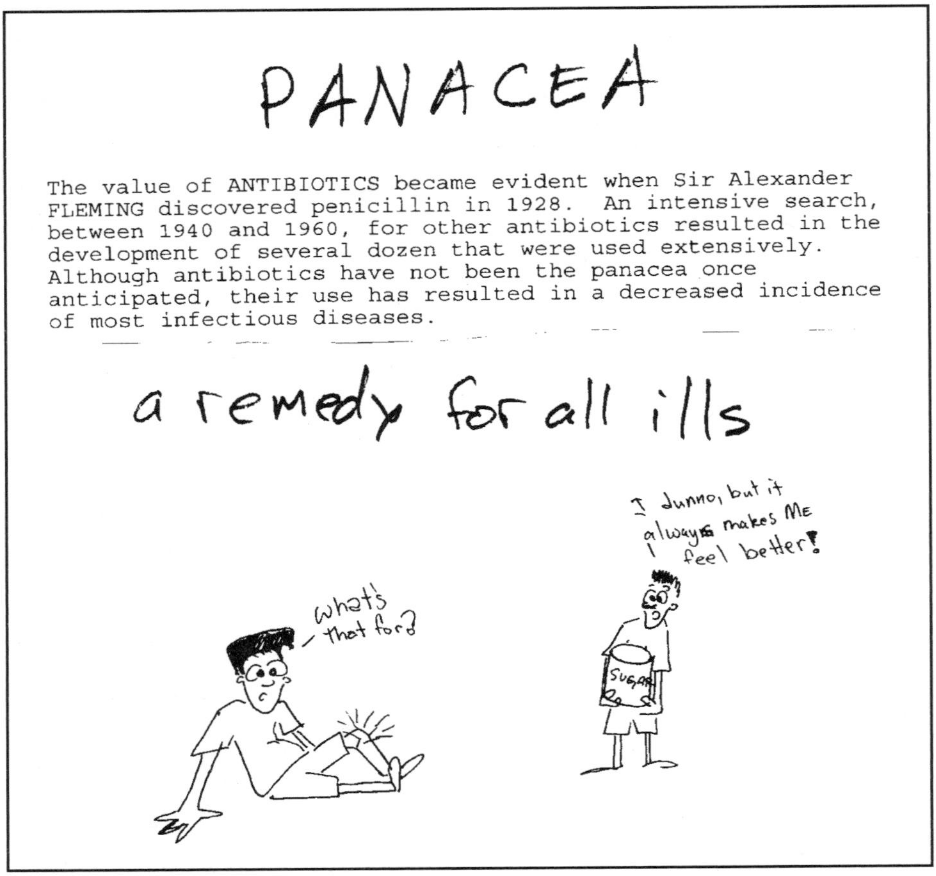

Figure 4.3

format to their class reading word lists. The son of a middle school assistant principal I know adapted the format for his journal as a way to learn new words (see Figure 4.3).

School and Classroom Libraries

n the second edition of *In the Middle* (1998), Nancie Atwell writes about the importance of classroom libraries. "A class-room library invites students to browse, chat, make recommendations to each other, select, reject, and generally feel at home with literature" (37). While most language arts teachers feel confident about choosing works of fiction for their school and classroom libraries, fewer of them feel qualified to choose informational texts: when it comes to nonfiction, they just aren't sure. A resource that has helped me evaluate texts is Freeman and Person's *Using Nonfiction Trade Books in the Elementary Classroom: From Ants to Zeppelins* (1992). This book has chapters on understanding the genre, evaluating and choosing books, and integrating them into the K–8 curriculum.

Some teachers don't like their students to read informational books during sustained silent reading because they think it's not the same kind of reading: "How do you count the pages they've read when informational books have all those pictures and things?" My response: "How should you assess engagement during SSR? Is it number of pages or authentic response?" Many content area teachers rely solely on the textbook because they are unaware of titles that support the information found there. Some teachers have no background in children's literature; others believe that literature belongs in the reading class. These problems add up to one result in many schools and classrooms: books that many students would find truly engaging, that would build specialized vocabulary knowledge, and that would help them find answers to their questions never find their way into the students' hands.

Informational books have incredible value in the classroom. In the fifth edition of *Through the Eyes of a Child* (1999), Norton says: "Remember that one of the greatest values in informational books is *enjoyment*" (693). While giving pride of place to enjoyment, she enumerates seven more quantifiable reasons information books are critical to our classroom libraries:

- They convey knowledge.
- They provide opportunities for children to experience the excitement of discovery.
- They introduce the scientific method (observation, comparison, formulation/testing of hypothesis, drawing conclusions).

- They encourage self-reliance.
- They encourage the mind to stretch.
- They encourage critical reading and thinking skills.
- They expand children's vocabularies by introducing new words and technical terms.

When informational books are balanced with quality fiction, the classroom library truly supports new word learning in magical ways. Moffett and Wagner's fourth edition of *Student-Centered Language Arts, K–12* (1992) recommends 112 kinds of literature to include in a classroom library. They range from rhymes and songs to recipes, from memoirs to parables. Had I used this list as I built my classroom libraries, I would have met the needs of all my readers in more effective ways.

Thousands of high-quality fiction and nonfiction books can be used to achieve the goals I've outlined for vocabulary instruction, but I'll offer a few examples in each content area (and in some special categories) as a way of indicating general strengths to look for. Most of the books in the categories below could be included in others as well—good books are good books no matter where they are read—but I've placed them under the headings in which I believe they offer the most support. Although I offer a few fiction suggestions for each area, the list is weighted in favor of informational books because of the rich, diverse vocabulary found there.

Art and Artists

David Macaulay's books (*Castle; Cathedral; Pyramid; Ship;* and *The Way Things Work*) have brought architecture into the hands of readers in intriguing ways. The language accompanying the illustrations is readable in part because of the visual detail. Each book has an incredible list of related, specialized words in the glossary.

The World of Theater (1995) which is part of Scholastic's *Voices of Discovery* series, introduces readers to the language of theater. Discussing everything from masks to makeup, types of drama to theater history, this intriguing book includes overlays, pop-ups, colorful illustrations, detailed drawings, and definitions.

Diane Stanley and Peter Vennema's *Charles Dickens: The Man Who Had Great Expectations* and *Bard of Avon: The Story of William Shakespeare* are meticulously researched and take us behind the scenes into the lives of these great authors. The language in them is rich, and unfamiliar terms are explained within the text. These books fit well with Kathleen Krull's *Lives of the Writers: Comedies, Tragedies, and What the Neighbors Thought; Lives of the Artists: Masterpieces, Messes, and What the Neighbors Thought;* and *Lives of the Musicians: Good Times, Bad Times, and What the Neighbors Thought.* Each artist has several pages devoted to him or her, beginning with a detailed caricature. Interesting tidbits combined with quotes from the artists make for interesting, memorable language. Each section ends with a "bookmark" that gives background information related to health, family life, and work. Again, the rich language, combined with a great deal of humor, helps engage the readers. An equally engaging behind-the-scenes picture is drawn by Zheng Zhensun and Alice Low in *A Young Painter: The Life and Paintings of Wang Yani—China's Extraordinary Young Artist.*

Ernest Raboff's *Art for Children* books make the art of specific artists understandable and accessible to beginning readers of any age. Each focuses on a single artist: Renoir, DaVinci, Rembrandt, Matisse, Picasso. The text is not easy to read but is highly accessible because of the supporting illustrations and reproductions of the artist's work. Words such as *harlequin, cubism,* and *etchings,* are explained, illustrated, and brought to life. Mark Venezia has done similar books on DaVinci and Van Gogh for even younger readers. The books are rich with detailed drawings, cartoons, reproductions, large print, and a thorough text that defines words readers probably won't know.

Health and Physical Education

Informational books in which teenagers tell their stories in their own words are extremely popular because of the personal connections students make to these stories. Janet Bode combines teenagers' stories with medical facts, statistics, and resources in a number of powerful collections: *Hard Time: A Real-Life Look at Juvenile Crime and Violence* (coauthored by Mack); *Trust and Betrayal: Real Life Stories of Friends and Enemies;* and *Death Is Hard to Live With: Teenagers Talk About How They Cope with Loss.* Michael Ford's collection *The Voices of AIDS: Twelve Unforgettable People Talk About How AIDS Has Changed Their Lives,* Random House's *CityKids Speak on Prejudice* (CityKids Foundation 1994), and Susan Kuklin's *Teenagers Take on Race, Sex, and Identity* are filled with strong voices representing a variety of cultures.

Bookstores are filled with informational books related to sports and physical conditioning. The *Sports Illustrated for Kids* series offers the latest biographies and updates of sports heroes as well as statistical information. Zander Hollander edits a collection of NBA facts each year, *The NBA Book of Fantastic Facts, Feats, and Superstats.* For many readers, understanding words like *spectacular, well-deserved,* and *affiliate* in the context of sports will improve their ability to transfer those words to other areas. Four collections of sports short stories are also excellent resources. Donald Gallo's *Ultimate Sports,* L. M. Schulman's *The Random House Book of Sports Stories,* Chris Crutcher's *Athletic Shorts,* and Geof Smith's *Above 95th Street and Other Basketball Stories* all provide the kind of reading that will hook some students. These short stories can foster a curiosity about reading that pushes students toward reading biographies, autobiographies, and novels related to sports.

Language Arts: Thinking About Words

An incredible number of books today are based on playing with language. Reading these books with students, figuring out the riddles and making up new ones, inventing language, coming up with words no one has ever heard, are only the beginning. Students quickly become addicted to the joy of this kind of word discovery. Lateral thinking puzzle books never fail, although you shouldn't keep them on your classroom shelves, because the solutions are included. Once students know the solution the challenge is gone. (Do you find it amazing that the same students who can't remember to bring a pen to class or even what you did in class yesterday can remember the solutions to all of these puzzles? Trust me; they can.) In any case, the puzzles are short and easily read aloud. Titles I have include: Brecker's *Lateral Logic Puzzles;* Sloan's *Test Your Lateral Thinking, Lateral Thinking Puzzlers, and Perplexing Lateral Thinking Puzzles;* and Sloane and MacHale's *The Lateral Logician.*

Several books emphasize grammar and parts of speech in very engaging ways. Ruth Heller's books are quite well known: *Mine, All Mine: A Book About Pronouns; A Cache of Jewels and Other Collective Nouns; Merry-Go-Round: A Book About Nouns;* and *Kites Sail High: A Book About Verbs.* Each page of Bill Martin, Jr. and Vladimir Radunsky's picture book *The Maestro Plays* describes the maestro's playing using a range of adverbs. Two recent additions to my collection are by Karen Elizabeth Gordon. Her *The Deluxe Transitive Vampire: The Ultimate Handbook of Grammar for the Innocent, the Eager, and the Doomed* explains pronoun-antecedent agreement this way: "Pronouns and their antecedents are made for each other. An *antecedent* itself is rarely on its own: there'll always be a possessive pronoun nearby, watching anxiously, flashing the wedding ring." Her *The New Well-Tempered Sentence: A Punctuation Handbook for the Innocent, the Eager, and the Doomed* describes the function of parentheses: "Parentheses pal around in pairs to enact their literal meaning taken from the Greek: a putting in beside. They make for a softer interruption than the abrupt snapping or darting that dashes do, and they find many situations where they feel at home." I laughed out loud reading these two remarkably informative and memorable books.

My copy of Jennie Maizels and Kate Petty's *The Amazing Pop-Up Grammar Book* has been stolen and returned many times. Each page focuses on a part of speech through pop-ups, humorous pictures, questions, and interactive activities. Fred Gwynne has entertained readers by challenging them to think about the visual that comes to mind when homonyms are mixed up. *A Chocolate Moose for Dinner, The King*

Who Rained, A Little Pigeon Toad, and *The Sixteen-Hand Horse* all have delightful illustrations that require the reader to think of the homonym that will make a well-known phrase make sense.

Studying the eccentric nature of language is a sure way to hook students into learning new words, and David Feldman's *Who Put the Butter in Butterfly? and Other Fearless Investigations into Our Illogical Language* is one book with which to introduce that study. Other examples include Norton Juster and Eric Carle's *Otter Nonsense;* Herbert Kohl's *A Book of Puzzlements;* Richard Lederer's *Crazy English, Anguished English, Literary Trivia,* and *Get Thee to a Punnery;* Levitt, Burger and Guralnick's *The Weighty Word Book;* Bruce and Brett McMillan's *Puniddles;* Giulio Maestro's *What's Mite Might?;* Nigel Rees's *The Phrase That Launched 1,000 Ships;* Norman Solomon's *The Power of Babble;* William Steig's *CDB!;* Murray Suid's *Demonic Mnemonics;* and Ruth Young and Mitchell Rose's *To Grill a Mockingbird and Other Tasty Titles.*

Looking at where words come from is also an interesting way for students to learn new words. In Margy Burns Knight's *Who Belongs Here? An American Story,* the author and illustrator tell two stories, that of Nary, a young boy who has escaped from Cambodia and lives in America, and one about how language in America has been enriched with each new wave of immigrants. (This is also an excellent resource for social studies classes studying immigration.) Check out Milton Meltzer's *A Book About Names: In Which Custom, Tradition, Law, Myth, History, Folklore, Foolery, Legend, Fashion, Nonsense, Symbol, Taboo Help Explain How We Got Our Names and What They Mean.* It covers a range of name-related information, from which names have been most popular to the ways Jewish people were required to change their names during the Holocaust.

Deborah Morris's *Real Kids, Real Adventures: Amazing True Stories of Young Heroes and Survivors Who Lived to Tell the Tale!* and Kathryn Kulpa's *Short Takes: Brief Personal Narratives and Other Works by American Teen Writers* offer students an opportunity to hear teenage voices using more sophisticated language. It is important that students hear their teachers using such language, of course, but encountering peers who use content-rich language is even more significant. It helps student writers give voice to their thoughts in language they previously might not have considered.

Math

Math informational books come in a variety of genres: picture books that require mathematical reasoning (e.g., Scieszka and Smith's *Math Curse* and the mathematical folktale adapted by David Barry, *The Rajah's Rice*), books that recreate a story using math (e.g., Mitsumasa Anno's *Anno's Magic Seeds, Anno's Mysterious Multiplying Jar, Socrates and the Three Little Pigs,* and *Anno's Hat Tricks*), and stories that teach mathematical concepts (e.g., Cindy Neuschwander's *Sir Cumference and the First Round Table: A Math Adventure*). These books convey mathematical information and specialized language that help students transfer word and concept knowledge to both textbook and real-life mathematical challenges. Biographies that highlight the thinking of famous mathematicians, Paul Hoffman's *The Man Who Loved Only Numbers: The Story of Paul Erdos and the Search for Mathematical Truth,* Bruce Schechter's *My Brain Is Open,* and Sylvia Nasar's *A Beautiful Mind* offer older, more fluent readers much more abstract and complex language as they explore a particular person's life and mind. So often we focus on the struggling reader, but it is important to remember that language acquisition continues at all ages and stages.

In an enchanting fantasy novel written by Wendy Isdell, *A Gebra Named Al,* Julie meets a gebra named Al and accompanies Al and the Periodic horses through the land of mathematics. Filled with math and science basics, this book will help students learn the specialized language of math. *Math Talk: Mathematical Ideas in Poems for Two Voices,* by Theoni Pappas, also invites students to play with and learn mathematical language. Poems with titles like "Fractals," "Fibonacci Numbers," and "Googols" are guaranteed to bring math language to life.

Science

Wendy Isdell's sequel to *A Gebra Named Al* is entitled *The Chemy Called Al* (though it is a sequel, it can be read independently). When her reading light goes out, Julie places her chemistry book under her head and finds herself in the land of science. The gas state, the liquid state, the solid state, and the elemental forest are all on the map. This delightful novel makes scientific language seem the stuff of everyday life.

J. Lynett Gillette's *Dinosaur Ghosts: The Mystery of Coelophysis* begins, "There is a saying that the place called Ghost Ranch in New Mexico got its name because each night after dark, its fossils come out of the ground to play." Who could resist this lead?

Poetry collections like Martha Paulos's *Insectasides,* Douglas Florian's *Insectlopedia,* and Paul Fleischman's *Joyful Noise* and *I Am Phoenix* immortalize insects and birds in rhyming poetry. They add to the specialized vocabulary and content knowledge that help students find answers to their questions and give language to their thinking and writing in science. Another book students love is Steve Parker's *Brain Surgery for Beginners and Other Major Operations for Minors: A Scalpel-Free Guide to Your Insides.* This book has extremely technical scientific language, but the humorous illustrations, short chunks of text, and intricately labeled charts all help readers understand the language. Books in the *Horrible Science* series (Nick Arnold's *Ugly Bugs* is one) give readers answers to previously unanswerable questions. And most adolescents delight in reading the disgusting facts put forth in Todd Strasser's *Kids' Book of Gross Facts and Feats.*

David Feldman's *Why Do Clocks Run Clockwise?* and *When Do Fish Sleep?* and Martin Goldwyn's *How a Fly Walks Upside Down and Other Curious Facts* all add to the scientific knowledge and word knowledge that so help students as they begin to apply scientific principles to their own life. Sterling publishes a series of interesting "experiment" books that help students internalize the three expository text structures primarily used in technical writing, textbooks, and standardized tests (problem/solution, cause/effect, and sequence): Louis Loeschnig's *Simple Earth Science Experiments, Simple Kitchen Experiments,* and Anthony Fredericks's *Simple Nature Experiments.*

Social Studies

Informational books for the social studies teacher abound. Margy Burns Knight's *Talking Walls* introduces readers to places and names associated with famous walls around the world. It uses words such as *Aborigines, descendants, pilgrimage, conical towers,* and *kivas* with illustrations as support. Bobbie Kalman's *Historic Communities* books (*Children's Clothing of the 1800s, Settler Sayings, Games from Long Ago, Customs and Traditions*) all provide historically accurate research information. The illustrations and vocabulary are particularly appropriate for readers in the upper intermediate grades.

Scholastic's "newspaper" books (Michael Johnstone's *The History News,* Scott Steedman's *The Egyptian News,* and Powell and Steele's *The Greek News*) all contain detailed information, along with interesting vocabulary and supportive illustrations. Each "newspaper" reports on sports, fashion, farming, religion, politics, building, explorations, during the specified time period. In humorous articles, editorials, advertisements, and art, readers learn about hieroglyphs, papyrus scrolls, oracles, and the cost of building the Parthenon. Russ Stewart's *Fact or Fiction* books focus on a specific topic: *Cowboys, Bandits, and Outlaws, Conquerors and Explorers, Spies and Traitors.* These books are loaded with interesting facts; intriguing words, events, and people; and significant historical background. Whether in a cover come-on like "The truth about outlaws, highwaymen, smugglers, and robbers from the bandit gangs of ancient China to the desperadoes of today" or in an article title like "Toothless Death Scurvy," readers are introduced to hundreds of words and concepts in a way that only whets their appetite for more.

There are also many illustrated informational books that are presented as narratives: Jim Murphy's *The Great Fire* and *A Young Patriot:*

The American Revolution as Experienced by One Boy and Scholastic's *If You Were There* series (Elizabeth Levy's *If You Were There When They Signed the Constitution,* Ann McGovern's *If You Sailed on The Mayflower in 1620,* Kay Moore's *If You Lived at the Time of the American Revolution*) are excellent examples. Scholastic also publishes the highly successful *Horrible Histories* series: Terry Deary's *The Rotten Romans* and *The Measly Middle Ages* are delightful combinations of cartoons, graphs and charts, narration, letters, and wanted posters that convey a vast amount of information about those periods.

Russell Freedman and Milton Meltzer each offer carefully researched books about particular time periods and events. Freedman's rich language and compelling stories are frequently augmented by photographs and reproductions of original art (see, for example, *Buffalo Hunt, An Indian Winter,* and *Children of the Wild West*). A Meltzer book I have especially enjoyed sharing with students is *The Amazing Potato: A Story in Which the Incas, Conquistadors, Marie Antoinette, Thomas Jefferson, Wars, Famines, Immigrants, and French Fries All Play a Part.* As the title makes clear, Meltzer presents a somewhat playful but historically accurate timeline of the influence of the potato in our lives. The book discusses everything from agricultural tools to types of potatoes. Another is *Cheap Raw Material: How Our Youngest Workers Are Exploited and Abused.* Terms like *muckrakers* and *progressives* come to life as Meltzer tells how people have brought appalling working conditions to public attention and worked to improve them.

Students often think they have nowhere to turn but to encyclopedias when they are researching the lives of famous people. Today there are many illustrated biographies appropriate for children and young adults that also include lists of references for further information on the historical period in which the person lived. Four excellent books in this category are Robert Coles's *The Story of Ruby Bridges,* William Miller's *Frederick Douglass: The Last Day of Slavery,* Diane Stanley's *Cleopatra,* and Rosemary Bray's *Martin Luther King, Jr.*

Historical connections from a variety of perspectives, including at least one from that of an adolescent, are represented in the Discovery

Enterprises *Perspectives on History* series. Each book provides primary source documents (letters, logs, transcripts, photographs, interviews, etc.) for a specific time period. For example, Cheryl Edwards gives readers multiple views of the New Deal in *The New Deal: Hope for the Nation*. Books such as Ellen Levine's *Freedom's Children: Young Civil Rights Activists Tell Their Own Stories* provide not only interesting historical narratives, but also specialized reference aids such as acronym lists and bibliographic notes. Resources like these help students learn specialized vocabulary related to historical events.

Magazines

Magazines written for adolescents build word and content knowledge; they also allow readers to see that expository text structures differ from narration. There are many such magazines; three that directly support social studies and science are *Time Machine: The American History Magazine for Kids, Sports Illustrated for Kids,* and *Science Court Investigations.*

Alphabet Books

We're used to thinking of alphabet books as being for young, emergent readers. While there are indeed many alphabet books of this type, there are also alphabet books written specifically for older readers. Some are content specific, such as Jerry Palotta's science-related books, and some are devoted to types of words or other categories. If you are just starting a collection for older readers, I recommend choosing those that relate to your content area. A few I have particularly enjoyed are Gerald Hausman's *Turtle Island ABC;* Rudyard Kipling's *How the Alphabet Was Made;* John Magel's *Dr. Moggle's Alphabet Challenge;* Rien Poortvliet's *The Book of the Sandman and the Alphabet of Sleep;* Jeanne and William Steig's *Alpha Beta Chowder;* Judith Viorst's *The Alphabet from Z to A;* and Mike Wilks's *The Ultimate Alphabet* and *The Annotated Ultimate Alphabet.*

These books are wonderful resources and great reads, but they also can be used as models. After students are familiar with the pattern, they can form groups and write alphabet books for chapters of their textbooks. For example, using an American history textbook, each group can take a different time period and create an illustrated alphabet book that represents words, people, and events of the period. (the fifties? "B is for beatniks, who had hair aplenty"; the sixties? "B is for bombs that fell in Vietnam"). Students will need to read their textbooks closely and consult supplementary resources in order to create their alphabet books. (They may need to interview people who lived during certain periods in order to fill in those difficult letters, *q, x,* and *z.*)

Learning words should be fun even when it is challenging. Taking time each week to enjoy language gives students the opportunity to explore words and idiomatic expressions in ways they would not have otherwise imagined. A few minutes spent with portmanteau words (words that blend two or more distinct forms: *smog, motel, dictaphone, telethon, brunch*) will soon have students exploring word etymology. Time spent reading aloud from poetry collections that represent other cultures (Agard and Nichols's edited collection *A Caribbean Dozen: Poems from Caribbean Poets*) or languages other than English (Carlson's edited collection *Cool Salsa: Bilingual Poems on Growing Up Latino in the United States*) helps students learn words connected to other cultures and languages.

Robert Coles, in *The Call of Stories* (1989), remembers when he and his brother sat and listened to their parents read to each other: "I can still remember my father's words as he tried to tell me, with patient conviction, that novels contain 'reservoirs of wisdom,' out of which he and my mother were drinking." We must make our classrooms reservoirs of wisdom—places where students want to drink again and again. Putting literature at the heart of vocabulary instruction makes the water more satisfying.

CHAPTER  FIVE

How Do We Know It's Working?

"The question is," said Alice, "whether you *can* make words mean so many different things."

"The question is," said Humpty Dumpty, "which is to be master—that's all."

Lewis Carroll, *Through the Looking Glass*

In traditional vocabulary assessment we have evaluated a student's word knowledge by giving a test. Most students still complain about those weekly vocabulary tests. I recently saw a great "Shoe" (Jeff MacNelly) cartoon: Shoe is seated at his desk, vocabulary test in hand; he looks at the word *Primogeniture*, obviously has no idea what the word means, and writes "Really good geniture" as his response.

Recently I talked with a group of middle school teachers about how we can rethink our methods of vocabulary instruction and assessment. One teacher spoke for many when she said, "I know you're going to say we shouldn't give tests, but I have to give tests. I have to know it's working." She was wrong; I wasn't going to say that vocabulary tests should never be given. I just wanted them to look at the range of options they had for "knowing it's working."

In Susan Ohanian's book *Ask Ms. Class* (1995, 168–69), a letter writer asks Ms. Class how to get a colleague to stop giving isolated vocabulary tests, which she feels don't go with believing in the importance of authentic reading. Ms. Class's reply begins:

> Ms. Class would advise that you be not so fond of censure. Ms. Class is not aware of either any religious commandment or a Constitutional Amendment on the topic of vocabulary quizzes.

Tests are one of many ways that teachers and students can assess the growing understanding of words they are learning. If vocabulary instruction changes, however, the tests must reflect a different way of thinking about language. Many teachers have made great strides in moving away from traditional look-it-up-and-write-it-in-a-sentence instruction. Their new strategies involve integration and meaningful use of words, repetition of words in multiple contexts, and opportunities for students to see and hear words as part of a rich reading program. Yet, when it comes time for the weekly vocabulary test, multiple-choice and fill-in-the-blanks continue to be the standard.

Baker, Simmons, and Kameenui (1995a) state, "Interventions to increase the vocabulary knowledge of diverse learners should move systematically toward ensuring that students become independent word learners." Assessment should be another step in moving students toward independence. One way to continue that process toward independence is to give students multiple opportunities and multiple ways to demonstrate their knowledge of words and concepts.

Concept Circles

I discovered concept circles in Richard and Jo Anne Vacca's *Content Area Reading* (1986). In this technique students are shown a circle, each quarter of which contains a word or phrase. The student must then describe or name the concept to which all the sections relate. In doing this, students have to determine the meaning of each of the words, analyze the connections among the words, and think of a concept or relationship that ties the words together. For example, I created the concept circle in Figure 5.1 when we finished reading Irene Hunt's *No Promises in the Wind*. I filled in the circle with words representing effects (hobo, Hoovervilles, Dust Bowl migrant) and my students had to come up with a concept that would be considered a cause in the Depression. The technique can also be

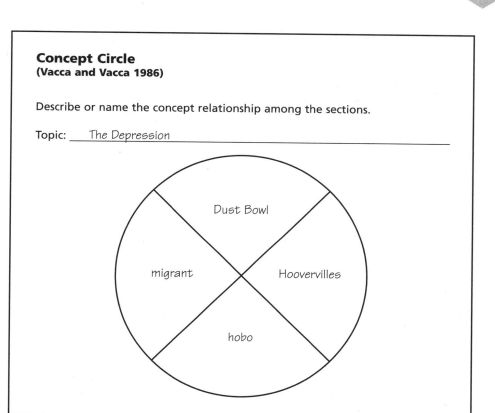

Concept Circle
(Vacca and Vacca 1986)

Describe or name the concept relationship among the sections.

Topic: _____The Depression_____

Dust Bowl

migrant

Hoovervilles

hobo

Figure 5.1

used in reverse. In Figure 5.2 I gave students the concept (the civil rights movement), and they had to complete the concept circle with four things they had learned in relation to this concept. This tool lets you ascertain the connections your students are able to make from their learning about a given concept.

Integration and Meaningful Use

Figure 5.3 lists some examples of assessment questions that match instruction based on integration and meaningful use. Sample questions 1, 2, and 4 require students to use

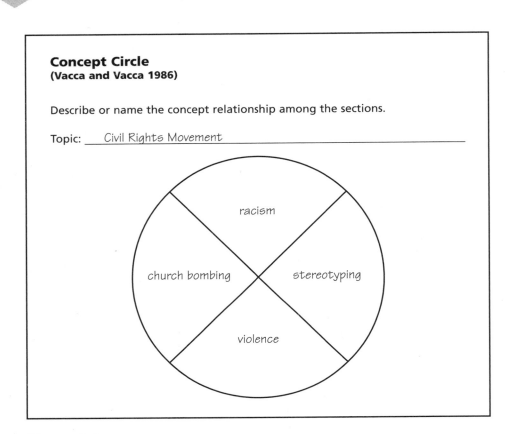

Concept Circle
(Vacca and Vacca 1986)

Describe or name the concept relationship among the sections.

Topic: _____Civil Rights Movement_____

Figure 5.2

inference. The others ask students to make word-to-concept connections. All the questions require students to connect the words to their own lives and thinking, and several ask students to give examples of their perceived use of the word. While these questions may take a bit more time to design and grade, they prompt a significant level of thinking. In addition, these tasks help students realize that there is no single definition for a word.

Figure 5.4 shows the way Ann Bailey now handles vocabulary exams for her middle school students in Long Beach, California. Her tasks and questions require students to think and write about the word, not just match definitions. The two students whose responses are shown here clearly have internalized word meanings, are able to dif-

Assessing Integration and Meaningful-Use Instruction

Single Definition   Inference
Sample 1
A jockey is a   cowboy   You would be most likely   racetrack
                  Wall Street worker to see a working jockey   cow ranch
                  horse racer   at a   sold house
                  furniture mover   post office

Sample 2
Read the following sentence and then answer the question that follows:
   *When the teacher heard that her student had stopped spending time with
   her usual friends, the teacher complimented her for making good choices.*
What do you think the teacher thought of her student's friends?

Sample 3
Four of our words this week were *adolescents, gangs, irresponsible,* and *irrational.* If I connect those four words by making this statement, "If you take a job where you work with adolescents, you can count on trouble with gangs, and on irresponsible and irrational behavior," I am guilty of doing what?

Sample 4
One of our target words this week was *preposterous.* What kind of in-school behavior would the principal think was preposterous?

Sample 5
The concept we discussed this week was *prejudice.* How could we use the prefix and the root word for this word to help us understand its meaning?

Sample 6
The concept we have been studying is *balance.* What might someone do who is trying to find balance in his life?

Sample 7
Four of our target terms this week were *pollution, population control, public transportation,* and *pesticides.* In what ways could all of these terms be connected to a larger concept?

Figure 5.3

ferentiate forms of the words, and can make personal connections to the meanings by giving examples. This form of testing gives a powerful message to students about the purpose of vocabulary instruction.

Follow directions for each numbered vocabulary word. Write with complete sentences. Use proper punctuation and capitalization. Make sure your handwriting is legible. **The vocabulary word must be used in your response.**

1. Describe a time you felt **queasy**. What caused the **queasiness**?

   I fell queasy when I went on a bus when I went to Mexico. I had a headache. What caused the queasiness is when it was hot in there and the bus was jumping.

2. What was the **zaniest** thing you ever did? How did others react when you were **zany**?

   What was the zaniest thing I did was I was acting goofy I was jumping around like a monkey, laughing for no reason and how the others react was, they were making weird faces and they left outside and start to laugh.

3. When were you ever in a **horde** of people or when did you see a **horde** of people? Describe the situation.

   I was in a horde one time because there was people fighting and there was a lot of people in the big circle and saying things like go jackson go Mariey bit him up and other things

4. Often, people must work **precisely**. On what occasions must you be **precise**? Why is **precision** required for you then?

   I must be precise to be in class ready to work before the bell rings. It is required for me because you have to get ready to learn about important things, mostly about new things that you never knew.

5. Describe something you have seen that is **moist**.

   the thing that was moist is rice. Cause when you cook the rice they need to have at least a little bit of water. So I need to be moist, enable to eat the rice. When rice is dry it won't taste good at all.

6. Why would your parents worry if you were **idle** too much of the time? What do you do during your **idle** time?

   they would worry because you need to learn how to do things enable to get a job, or a wife/husband, during idle time I would just sit down and watch tv.

Figure 5.4

Opposites

I adapted this activity from a Newspapers in Education workshop I attended a few years ago. I give the students a list of paired words with opposite meanings, and they scour a stack of newspapers to find and cut out pictures or cartoons that could represent the words. They then glue the pictures onto a grid (Figure 5.5 shows part of the grid). (If you use this activity, you'll need to provide multiple copies of newspapers, markers, scissors, glue sticks, and chart paper.) On the five rows of five squares each, the center square is free, and the bottom middle square is to be filled in with an example of the students' choosing.

You may need to remind students that they are not looking for the actual words; rather, they are looking for examples of the word in use. (*Common* might be a picture of people walking or jogging in a park; *unique* might be a picture of a mother and father with sixteen children.)

I have never seen this activity fail. It is a great tool for social studies and can also be very successful with English-as-a-second-language

Figure 5.5

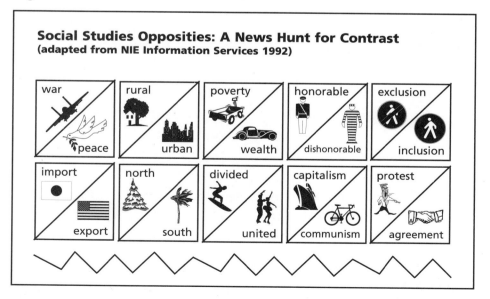

students (using words such as *early, late; high, low; empty, full; fast, slow*). Students (and teachers) of all ages quickly become absorbed in reading the newspaper and looking for examples of the pairs of opposites. Groups argue over the best examples and often change what they have chosen when they find a better example. This is an incredible tool for assessing whether students actually have a working knowledge of particular words. You can use words from your wordstorming or list–group–label lists. You can also give students one of the words and ask them to create the opposite.

Tausha Madden and Gail Sherman, language arts teachers at Glenridge Middle School in Orlando, Florida, use the "opposites" news hunt to assess students' understanding of words (*diligent, mundane, embellish, astute, unobtrusive, repugnant,* for example) in the literature they are reading. After teaching the words with explicit strategies like those described in Chapter 3, they ask their students to illustrate or find illustrations for the opposite of each word. This activity requires several levels of critical thinking and is an excellent way for students to demonstrate their creativity as well. Another extension of this idea would be for students to use computer clip art to create their pairs of opposites.

The Magic Square

The "magic square" has been around for many years. An alternative to the typical matching exercise, the magic square is an enjoyable way to assess an initial understanding of words and concepts. To make a magic square, begin by drawing up a two-column list: one column is a lettered list of terms; the other column is a numbered list of definitions. The size of the square is based on the number of terms used: 3 by 3 for 9 terms, 4 by 4 for 16 terms (as in Figure 5.6). Students match the definitions to the terms and place the number of the definition in the box bearing the letter of the term. (In Figure 5.6, for example, the A box contains the number 16, the definition of *affirmative action*.) Students are able to check the

Magic Square

Directions: Select from the numbered statements the best answer for each of the social studies terms. Put the number in the proper space in the magic square box. The total (sum) of the numbers will be the same across each row (horizontally) and down each column (vertically). Does it work diagonally on each axis of the "X" in the middle?

History Terms
A. affirmative action
B. Cold War
C. carpetbagger
D. expansionism
E. détente
F. impeach
G. hippie
H. fascism
I. nonrenewable resources
J. Solidarity
K. suffrage
L. perestroika
M. internment camp
N. yellow journalism
O. sanctions
P. McCarthyism

Statements
1. policy of falsely accusing people of working against the government
2. time of peaceful relations between U.S. and U.S.S.R.
3. irreplaceable natural resources
4. desire to gain more land
5. political and economic struggle between U.S. and U.S.S.R. from 1945 to 1989
6. the right to vote
7. a person in the 60s and 70s who questioned the established culture in the U.S. (what's your definition?)
8. sensationalized news stories written to sell papers
9. what rebels called Yankees who came south during reconstruction to get rich, usually unethically
10. labor union that helped end communism in Poland
11. charge a government leader with a crime
12. method used by nations to force a country to change
13. place where U.S. government held Japanese American citizens hostage during WWII
14. totalitarianism marked by right-wing dictatorship
15. the opening up of Soviet economy during 1980s
16. government requirement for schools and business to set aside positions for minorities

Answer Box

A	B	C	D
16	5	9	4
E	F	G	H
2	11	7	14
I	J	K	L
3	10	6	15
M	N	O	P
13	8	12	1

Magic Number =

Figure 5.6

accuracy of their matches, because correct matches will yield the same numerical total for each row across and down. If a given row doesn't add up to the magic number, students have made an error in matching words and definitions. In Figure 5.6, created by Anne Cobb, the magic number (the total of each horizontal and vertical column) is 34. While students (and teachers) enjoy this activity and find it a helpful way for reinforcing, checking, and testing knowledge of words, the magic square is time-consuming to construct unless you follow a template. Vacca and Vacca's *Content Area Reading* (1986, 325–26) offers eight alternative magic square combinations.

The assessment of vocabulary instruction should be varied and meaningful. Students need ways to ascertain both their ability to determine the meaning of unfamiliar words and to demonstrate their knowledge of words at the heart of an instructional unit. Some time should also be spent teaching students strategies for taking standardized tests that may require single definitions.

Most of the graphic organizers in Chapter 3 could also be used as assessment tools. Milner and Milner note that the public's ire over low SAT scores has caused secondary English teachers to follow a one-dimensional approach to vocabulary strength, which may divert English teachers from some better ways to improve the vocabulary of adolescents. While there is disagreement over whether SAT scores have actually dropped (*Reading Today* reports that "scores on the SAT this year [1998] remained steady, despite an increasingly diverse test-taking population" [12]), there is ample evidence that all our students need to spend more time with words and that teachers need to devise more authentic ways of assessing language growth. Whatever assessment you choose, moving students into roles that require them to recognize words, think about ways the words could be used in multiple contexts, and write about their personal connections to the words will be a step forward in helping them become independent word learners.

Are there ways other than tests or alternative assessments that students complete that will help us evaluate the balanced program we have put in place? I believe so. The assessment issue is much more complex than a single measurement that elicits a numerical score. In *Children of Promise: Literate Activity in Linguistically and Culturally Diverse Classrooms* (1991, 50), Heath and Mangiola summarize thus: "To build on the riches of diverse language forms and uses depends on relinquishing our previously held positions. The basic stuff of human learning—behaviors, motivations, and intentions—cannot be 'standardized' or measured, for psychological, social, and cultural 'laws' shed their predictability with altered contexts." Given that the very goal of vocabulary instruction is an "altered context"—we want students to increase their ability to transfer word knowledge from one context to another—single measures that are context bound don't work very well.

The more I read about vocabulary instruction and language acquisition, the more I am aware of the complexities that make learning language so challenging. For so many years, I sat in classrooms (both as a student and as a teacher) and walked away with the notion that words and meanings were easily learned and regurgitated. (I must say I slept better at night believing that naïve notion.) Now I know that although word definitions may be easily regurgitated, that is not learning. So, what are some big-picture ways whereby we can tell whether our vocabulary program is working? When we balance teacher-mediated word-learning strategies with time for reading, we should begin to see the following characteristics of both individual and whole-class behavior:

- An increased sense of word play.
- A heightened awareness of how words sound (rhyme, repetitive language patterns).
- An inquisitiveness about word meanings and derivations.
- A more diverse and richer use of language in speech and writing.
- An ability to construct semantic maps and graphic organizers to extend an understanding of words and concepts.
- An interest in word games (computers, board games, puzzles).
- An ability and willingness to read more complex literature.

These broad assessments won't give us numbers we can put in our grade book, but they do remind us that our work is larger than the numbers we are required to produce.

Baumann and Kameenui (1991) end their synthesis of the research by restating the quotation from Voltaire with which they began: "'Language is very difficult to put into words.' However, as educators, we find the reciprocal of Voltaire's statement even more challenging: Words are indeed very difficult to put into language (instruction)." I have written this book to support teachers who want to change the way they teach vocabulary, their goal being to help their students understand what they read and speak and write more fluently and eloquently.

I've long admired Zemelman, Daniels, and Hyde's *Best Practice* (1993), in which they cite research and then note areas in which we can increase one kind of instructional behavior and decrease another kind in order to bring practice more closely into alignment with that research. I've decided to follow that format here: to highlight practices we might decrease while increasing other practices in order to improve the word-learning done by our students (see Figure 5.7). These vocabulary "best practices" are characterized by more reading, more concept development, explicit instruction for critical and specialized terms, increased opportunities to hear and use language in meaningful ways, and assistance in transferring that learning to other contexts. Ineffectual instructional practices move students away from seeing words as multifaceted sources of enjoyment and information.

What do students who have spent several years learning words in more traditional ways think when their teachers change the way they teach vocabulary? Ann Bailey's middle school students wrote letters to me after Ann and her team members started using new strategies to teach vocabulary. I'd like to quote from these letters as a reminder that children and their opinions are at the heart of all that we do. Richard Iannelli, in *The Devil's New Dictionary: Diabolic Definitions for Our Times*, defines the word *read* as follows: "to enter the world of the word, where the mind is monarch, where the boundaries are horizons yet unseen, and where time

---

Developing Effective Practices in Vocabulary Instruction

Increase	Decrease
• Time for reading	• Looking up definitions as a single source of word knowledge
• Use of varied, rich text	• Asking students to write sentences for new words before they've studied the word in depth
• Opportunities for students to hear or use words in natural sentence contexts	
• Use of concrete contexts when possible (pictures, artifacts)	• Notion that all words in a text need to be defined for comprehension
• Opportunities for students to use words in meaningful ways	• Using context as a highly reliable tool for increasing comprehension
• Opportunities for students to connect new words/concepts to those already known	• Assessments that ask students for single definitions
• Study of concepts rather than single, unrelated words	
• Explicit concept instruction and incidental encounters with words	
• Teaching strategies leading to independent word learning	
• Finding the word or concept that will have the biggest impact on comprehension rather than "covering" many words superficially	
• Opportunities for inference	

Figure 5.7

is an ocean as swift as a river and as still as a lake." Ann's students have definitely entered into the "world of the word." I hope you enjoy their words on the importance of vocabulary as much as I do:

- I like your ideas especialy the one with multible choice. I don't like the other ones.
- I am 12 years old but I am short. And I am learning some words and it is fun.
- You need vocabulary so you can use bigger words. You use big words like groan-up words. Once you grow up and get a job your boss

might use some of the big words and you might not understand.

- No, I never use any word that is in my vocabulary.

- I think all of us like [words in context] best. We learn more and more words every day. Just to get us warmed up its neat. At the end of the year we will have 120 words in our vocabulary.

- Thank you for teaching our teachers the stuff you taught them. I use all the words we do in my writing or like when I'm talking to someone.

- During these last few weeks as I did the vocabulary activity I thought to myself this is an activity that helps me a lot and it helps me with my reading also.

- I think the best way I learned new vocabulary words is the context one. Where you put the word and put the definition. You give examples and examples that are not the same as the word. I think that is a great way to learn vocabulary words. You get to ask questions and talk about it.

- Every day I learn new words I never knew like awe, horde and zany. I never knew these words and now I know that zany is a crazy idea, horde is a crowd of people, and awe means awesome and wonderment.

Changing the way we teach is always a risk. There are always moments when we wonder if what we have decided to do is really an improvement over what we have been doing. Even when the evidence indicates that our past practice has been ineffective, it is often difficult to try something new. And when we try the "something new," it is difficult to stay with these new practices when we encounter difficulty or resistance, especially if that resistance is coming from students who don't want to change. Caine and Caine (1994, 106) offer one reason that it is so easy for us to revert to traditional practices even when we have evidence that those practices are not productive. "One of the most dramatic conclusions that flow from the brain theories is that threat affects those deep meanings that are dominant. When we are threatened, we downshift into more automatic beliefs and practices."

A couple of years ago I saw a freeway sign in Los Angeles that said, "When you're through changing, you're through." Perhaps, like most of our practices that eventually turn into something sound and effective, the key is that constant change—a process of trial, reflection, reseeing, and trying again. We may still downshift, but we'll do it less often and with greater resistance.

Last year a group of middle school teachers whose students had extremely low scores on their state-mandated reading tests asked me, "But if we change the way we're teaching, can you guarantee that our students will do better." I quoted Susan Ohanian, in *Ask Ms. Class,* "On a good day the best you can hope for is the students might." I also reminded them that these same students' scores had dropped drastically and consistently during their time at this middle school—serious confirming evidence that what they had been doing was not working. They decided to begin a process for rethinking: one of the teachers said, "Janet is right. What harm could it do?" A dubious reason, perhaps, but it got them started.

I'd like to conclude by quoting a student from a middle school classroom here in Florida, where I live and teach. The teachers in this school had been reluctant to implement the strategies I've discussed here, so I asked one of the teachers to ask her students what they thought about the way they were learning new words. The following response left us both laughing and left her willing to try something new: "Learning vocabulary is like a rotten turd."

I saw a poster today that said, "When you do what you've always done, you'll be where you've always been." Our students give us ample reasons to take a risk and try something we haven't done before—especially those who characterize our instruction in manure terms! Tom Booker, in *The Horse Whisperer,* highlights the goal of vocabulary instruction:

> Books had a kind of magic. But these teachers here, with all their talk, well. . . . Seems to me if you talk about these things too much, the magic gets lost and pretty soon talk is all there is. Some things in life just . . . are.

I hope this book helps you discover that teaching vocabulary can be one of the most enjoyable aspects of your school day—a time that leaves you and your students hungry for the magic we find in books.

A

Research and Resources for More Information on Vocabulary

Adams, D., and C. Cerqui. 1989. *Effective Vocabulary Instruction.* Kirkland, WA: Reading Resources.

This book begins with several pages highlighting research on effective practices in vocabulary instruction. Most classroom teachers will be drawn to the many graphic organizers and suggestions for classroom practice offered in the remainder of the book. Each of the instructional techniques is based on reading-style research. I adapted "Word in Context" and "How Well Do I Know These Words" from this book.

Baker, S. K., D. C. Simmons, and E. J. Kameenui. 1995a. *Vocabulary Acquisition: Curricular and Instructional Implications for Diverse Learners.* Technical Report No. 13. University of Oregon: National Center to Improve the Tools of Educators.

This technical report is designed to aid educators who have found that "although vocabulary development pervades every subject from reading mathematics to physical education, it is difficult to isolate for instructional purposes." As a way of synthesizing the research, the authors examine the instructional implications in five areas they label "Big Ideas." These are conspicuous strategies, strategic integration, mediated scaffolding, primed background knowledge, and judicious review.

Baker, S., D. Simmons, and E. Kameenui. 1995b. *Vocabulary Acquisition: Synthesis of the Research.* Technical Report No. 13. University of Oregon: National Center to Improve the Tools of Educators.

At the foundation of this technical report is the research that demonstrates that "building knowledge requires more than accumulating facts about specific elements such as word definitions." Research synthesis supports improvement in beginning reading instruction; engagement in significant amounts of independent reading; understanding that directly teaching word meanings does not adequately reduce the gap between students with poor and rich vocabularies; and knowledge that words can and should be learned at different levels of understanding.

Baumann, J., and E. Kameenui. 1991. "Research on Vocabulary Instruction: Ode to Voltaire." In J. Flood, J. Jensen, D. Lapp, and J. Squire (eds.). Handbook on Teaching the English Language Arts, 604–32. New York: Macmillan.

This chapter synthesizes empirical research related to vocabulary knowledge and instruction. Exploring what we know and what we still need to learn about vocabulary knowledge, Bauman and Kameenui examine research related to word knowledge, the relationship between word knowledge and reading comprehension, and the relationship between vocabulary research and curriculum and instruction. From a teaching perspective, the highlight of the chapter is in the final pages where Bauman and Kameenui offer ten guiding principles for making instructional decisions.

Green, J. 1993. *The Word Wall: Teaching Vocabulary Through Immersion.* Ontario: Pippin.

This book offers the teacher an opportunity to examine specific lesson plans centered around the use of a word wall. Describing activities ranging from those involving dolch words, initial consonants, and phonics to synonym/antonym study, this book encourages teachers to immerse students in language.

Harmon, J. 1998. "Vocabulary Teaching and Learning in a Seventh-Grade Literature-Based Classroom." *Journal of Adolescent and Adult Literacy* 41, 7: 518–29.

This recent article describes the variety of vocabulary learning episodes Harmon documented in a six-month qualitative study of a middle school, literature-based classroom. The specific practice examples detailed serve as excellent support for those teachers who are trying to establish that there is substantial vocabulary instruction in a successful reading workshop format.

Johnson, D., ed. 1986. *Journal of Reading* 29, 7. Newark, DE: International Reading Association.

This entire issue of the *Journal of Reading* addresses issues related to vocabulary instruction. Articles range from the theoretical to the practical. Articles are built on the foundation that word knowledge is an integral component of reading comprehension and therefore offers support for enhancing that connection.

Nagy, W. 1988. *Teaching Vocabulary to Improve Reading Comprehension.* Urbana, IL: NCTE and Newark, DE: IRA.

This is one of the best resources available for examining both the research and practice of teaching vocabulary. In spite of the fact that the book is only forty pages long, the research is synthesized in a remarkable way and the vocabulary strategies are extremely usable.

Quotations for Word Lovers

You will have written exceptionally well if, by skilful arrangement of your words, you have made an ordinary one seem original.

Horace, 65–8 B.C., *Ars Poetica*

So all my best is dressing old words new, Spending again what is already spent.

Shakespeare, 1564–1616, *Sonnet 76*

Of every four words I write, I strike out three.

Nicholas Boileau, 1636–1711, *Satire (2)*

A word fitly spoken is like apples of gold in pictures of silver.

Bible, Proverbs 25:11

Language is fossil poetry.

Ralph Waldo Emerson, 1803–1882, *Essays. Second Series (1844) "The Poet"*

A definition is the enclosing of a wilderness of idea within a wall of words.

Samuel Butler, 1835–1902, *Notebooks (1912)*

The limits of my language mean the limits of my world.

Ludwig Wittgenstein, 1889–1951, *Tractatus Logico-Philosophicus* (1922)

A phrase is born into the world both good and bad at the same time.
The secret lies in a slight, an almost invisible twist.
The lever should rest in your hand, getting warm, and you can
only turn it once, not twice.

Isaac Babel, 1894–1940, *Guy de Maupassant* (1932)

Slang is the language that rolls up its sleeves, spits on its hands and
goes to work.

Carl Sandburg, 1878–1967, in *The New York Times* 13 February 1959

A poem should not mean
But be.

Archibald MacLeish, 1892–1982, *"Ars Poetica"* (1926)

In our language rhyme is a barrel. A barrel of dynamite.
The line is a fuse. The line smoulders to the end and explodes;
and the town is blown sky-high in a stanza.

Vladimir Mayakovsky, 1893–1930, *"Conversation with an Inspector of Taxes About Poetry"*

Proverbs

Actions speak louder than words.

Fine words butter no parsnips.

One picture is worth a thousand words.

Practice what you preach.

Talk is cheap.

Word Games in the Classroom

Balderdash

Produced by Gameworks Creations, Inc. through Western Publishing Company, Inc., Racine, WI 53404, distributed by Games Gang Ltd., New York, NY 10010.

Played like the parlor game dictionary. Players create phony but believable definitions for given words and earn points for selecting the correct definition or if their "bluff" definition is selected. Great for assessing suffix, prefix, and root word knowledge.

Boggle

Produced by Parker Brothers, P.O. Box 1012, Beverly, MA 01915.

The "three-minute word game" in which players decipher words from a sixteen-letter cube tray, spelling any word diagonally, horizontally, vertically, or snakily formed in the tray. If the letters are connected, they will spell—longer words are rewarded with more points. This game has the advantage of being quick and allowing everyone to play at once.

Charades

Produced perhaps in some royal parlor or maybe even some fire-lit cave.

Get that kinesthetic energy and dramatic expression working in your vocabulary favor! Use vocab words, history terms, geometric shapes, famous names, places, or things—words from any content area can be used in this improvisational technique.

Listen Up!

Produced by The Game Works, Inc. under license from Steven Stroh, Inventor.

"Say what you see, draw what you hear." You've seen this premise before—you see a collection of lines, angles, and arcs on a card and must describe verbally what you see accurately enough for your partner to duplicate your words in picture. Great for math and science vocab—shapes, angular degrees, and fun.

Outburst

Produced by Parker Brothers, a division of Tonka Corporation, Beverly, MA 01915, under license from Hersch and Company.

Players are given a topic, such as "commands you give your dog" and then have sixty seconds to identify the ten listed on the playing card. This "game of verbal explosions" is played in teams.

Oodles

Produced by Milton Bradley Company, Springfield, MA 01101, a division of Hasbro, Inc.

Teams of players try to guess words beginning with a given letter, based on catchy clues. For example, the letter is B—"tiny mistake, or Yogi's buddy" (Boo Boo), "the deer politicians love to pass" (buck).

Password

Produced by Milton Bradley Company, Springfield, MA 01101.

Played like the old TV game show, players give one-word clues to guide their partners to the target word. Great for antonym and synonym play, also to assess vocabulary comprehension.

Pictionary

Produced by Western Publishing Company, Inc., Racine, WI 53404, distributed by the Games Gang, Ltd., New York, NY 10010.

Pictionary is literally charades on paper. Players identify unknown words through sketches. A one-minute time limit and a race around the board make for great word play through tactile translations, the "game of quick draw."

Probe

Produced by Parker Brothers, a division of General Mills Fun Group, Inc., Salem, MA 01970.

Played much like hangman, players choose a word, record it on a word tray, and expose letters as they are guessed, ultimately attempting to guess the word. Great for phun with fonemic awareness.

Scattergories

Produced by Milton Bradley Company, Springfield, MA 01101, a division of Hasbro.

This "fast-thinking categories game" combines the critical thinking strategy of categorization with word knowledge and beginning sounds. Players list words beginning with a specific letter in a given category. Points are earned only for those words no one else lists.

Scrabble

Manufactured by Selchow and Righter Company, Bay Shore, NY 11706.

If you don't know this one, ask your grandma. It's been on the market since 1948 and continues to make word play popular and fun.

Taboo

Produced by Milton Bradley Company, Springfield, MA 01101, a division of Hasbro, Inc.

Played in teams; players try to get their team to say the secret word, but there is a list of words that are taboo and cannot be spoken in the attempt. Great way to encourage your students to become on-the-spot thesauruses.

Win, Lose, or Draw

Produced by Milton Bradley Company, Springfield, MA 01101, a division of Hasbro, Inc.

Played just like Pictionary, only with familiar phrases instead of individual words. Based on the TV game show.

Word Yahtzee

Produced by E. S. Lowe, a Milton Bradley Company, Springfield, MA 01101.

Played like the popular numbers game, only with letters. "Roll the dice, build words and score big!"

Prefixes, Roots, and Suffixes

Prefix	Meaning	Examples
a, an	not or without	atypical, atrophy, anonymous
ab	away from, off	absent, abstain, abandon
ad	to	admit, adept, addict
amphi	both, around	amphibious, amphitheater
bene	well, good	benefit, benefactor, benign
co	together	cohabitant, cooperate, coordinate
dis	opposite	dishonest, disagree, disgust
e, ex	out	exit, elusive, evacuate, extinguish
im, in	not	impossible, inevitable
in	with	insight
mal	bad, badly	malign, malignant, malicious
mis	wrongly, bad	mistake, misconception
pre	before	preview, preamble, prefix
re	back, again	revoke, review, regard
sub	under	submarine, subject, submerge
super	above, beyond	superficial, superintendent
trans	across	transcend, transport, translate
un	not	unreal, unable, unfounded

Root	Meaning	Examples
acri, acer	sharp, bitter	acrid, acute, acid
act	do	action, react, enact
amicus	friend	amicable, amiable
aud	hear	audience, auditorium, audible
cred	believe	credit, incredible, discredit
chron	time	chronology, synchronize, chronicle
dic	speak	predict, dictate, contradict
flu	to flow	fluent, superfluous, affluent
fid	trust, have faith	fidelity, confidant, diffident
greg	flock, herd	congregate, segregate
luc, lumen	light	lucid, elucidate, luminous
pathos	feeling	apathy, sympathy, empathy
pug	fist	pugilist, repugnant
plac	make calm	placate, placid, complacent
spec, spic	to see, observe	conspicuous, perspective, spectacle
tract	pull, drag	tractor, distract, contract
vid	see	video, provide, evidence

Suffix	Meaning	Examples
able	able to	portable, curable, believable
ac	related to	maniac, cardiac, insomniac
acy, acity, acious	having the quality of	democracy, tenacity, vivacious
cide	to kill or cut	homicide, genocide, incision
cle, cule	small	particle, miniscule, molecule
crat	to rule	democrat, aristocrat
ee, eer	one who	employee, volunteer, auctioneer
en	to make	weaken, harden, loosen
er	more	wiser, harder, stronger
escent	becoming	adolescent, convalescent
est	most	wisest, hardest, strongest
ice	act of, time of	service, justice, novice
kin	little, small	napkin, manikin, munchkin
less	without	fearless, careless, hopeless
let	little	booklet, bracelet
logy, ology	study of	biology, psychology
ly	having the quality of	manly, motherly, miserly
ment	state, quality, act	excitement, basement, statement
ness	state, quality	kindness, happiness, friendliness
or	one who	donor, orator, tractor
ory, orium	place where	observatory, planetarium, factory

E.1 Research-Based Teaching

If this is the research 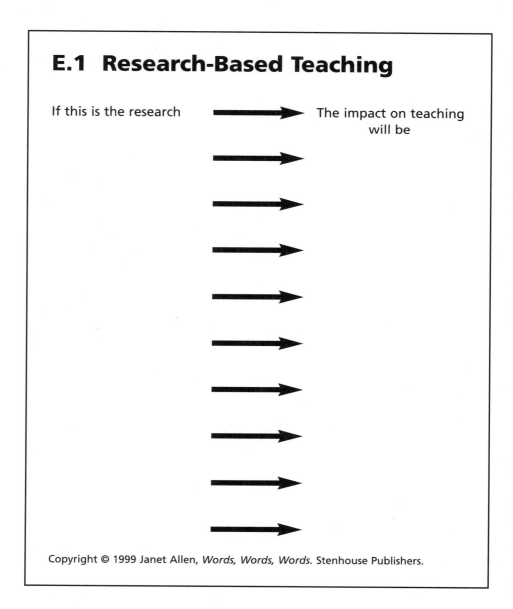 The impact on teaching will be

125

E.2 "Rich" or "Lean" Contexts

Rich Context	Lean Context

E.3 How Well Do I Know These Words?

Title: _____

Directions: First, read the words at the bottom of the page silently. After you read each one, write the words from the bottom of this page in the column that best describes what you know about each one.

Don't know at all	Have seen or heard—don't know meaning	I think I know the meaning	I know a meaning

E.4 How Well Do I Know These Words?

Title: _____

Directions: As I read the words listed below in the context of the story, you and your partner should decide if you know a meaning for the word that would fit the context. List the word, and your guess for the meaning of the word if you think or know that you know it, under the appropriate column.

I still need help finding a meaning for this word	I think I know the meaning	I know a meaning

E.5 From the New to the Known

This word is totally new to me	I've heard or seen this word, but I'm not sure what it means	I know one definition or could use this word in a sentence	I know several ways this word could be used

E.6 Concept Attainment

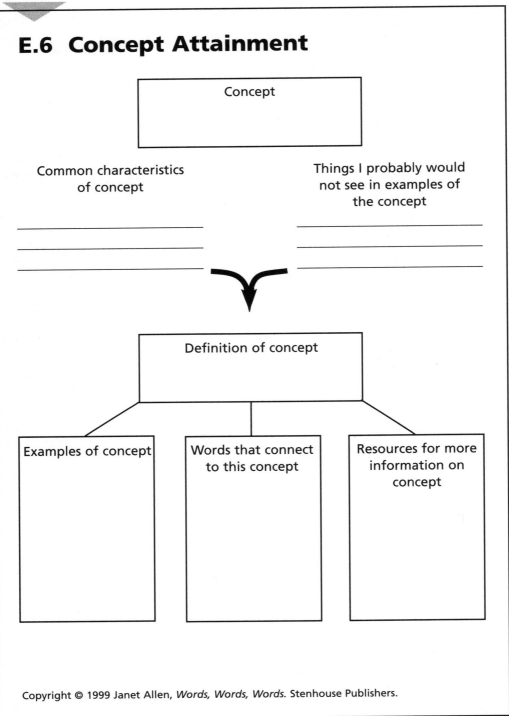

Concept

Common characteristics
of concept

Things I probably would
not see in examples of
the concept

Definition of concept

Examples of concept

Words that connect
to this concept

Resources for more
information on
concept

E.7 Concept Ladder
(Gillet and Temple 1982)

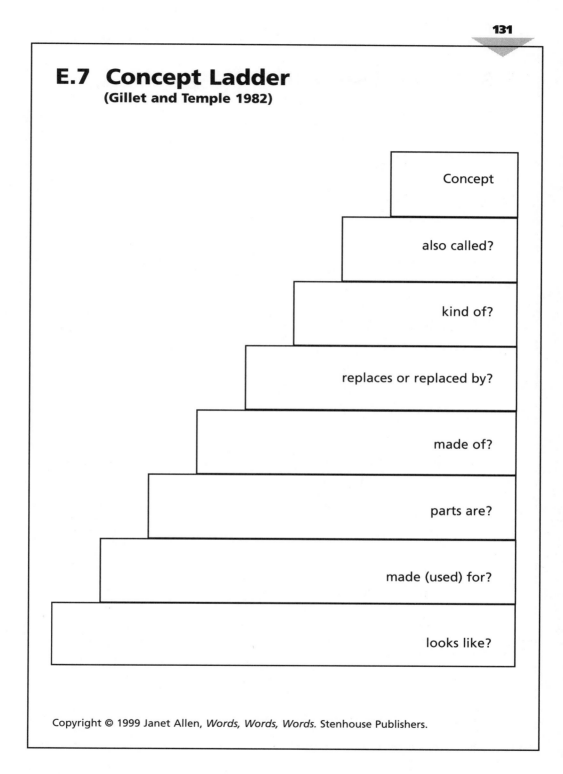

E.8 Making Connections

Using Associations to Develop Deeper Levels of Understanding

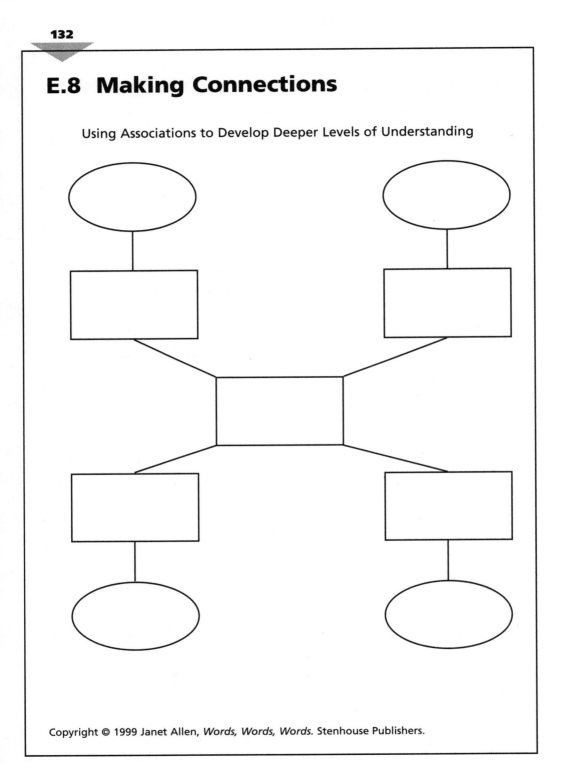

E.9 Understanding a Concept

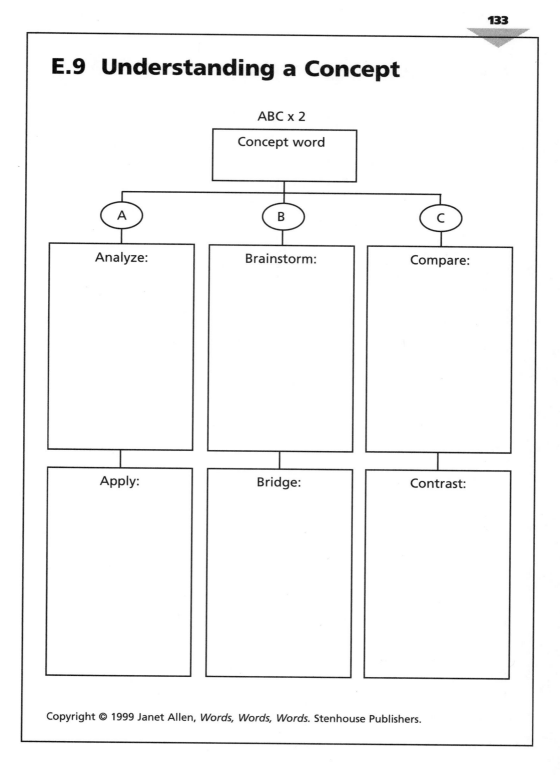

ABC x 2

Concept word

A   B   C

Analyze: Brainstorm: Compare:

Apply: Bridge: Contrast:

Copyright © 1999 Janet Allen, *Words, Words, Words.* Stenhouse Publishers.

E.10 Knowledge Chart

Word: _____

Prior knowledge about _____	New knowledge about _____

E.11 Analysis Map

Word or name

_____

Define or rename

_____

_____

Compare to: Contrast with:

_____   _____
_____   _____
_____   _____
_____   _____
_____   _____
_____   _____
_____   _____
_____   _____

Examples

_____

_____

_____

_____

E.12 Context → Content → Experience

Context: _____

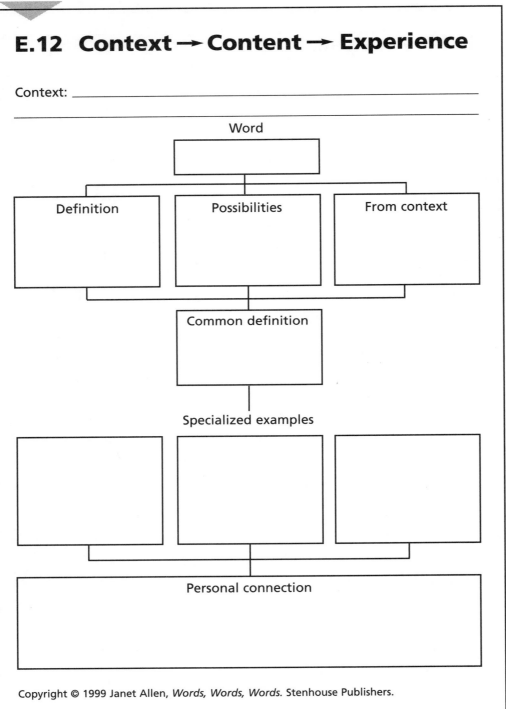

Word

Definition

Possibilities

From context

Common definition

Specialized examples

Personal connection

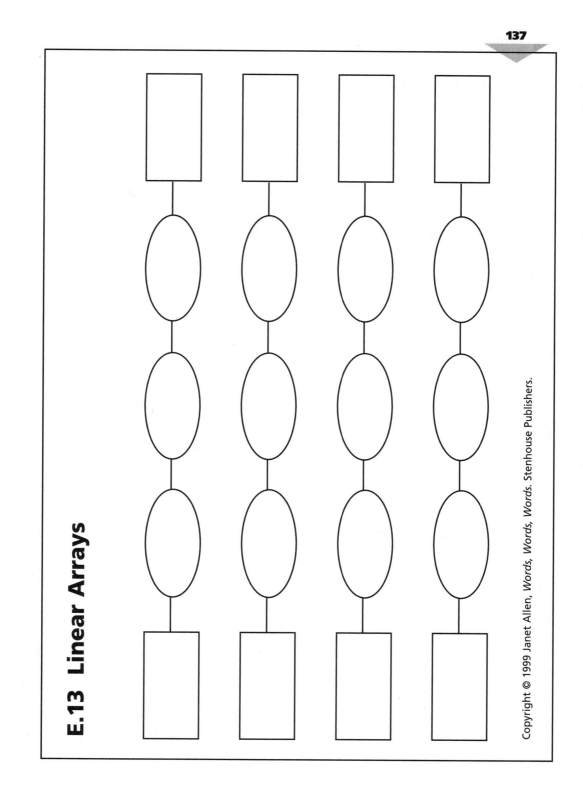

E.13 Linear Arrays

E.14 Part to Whole

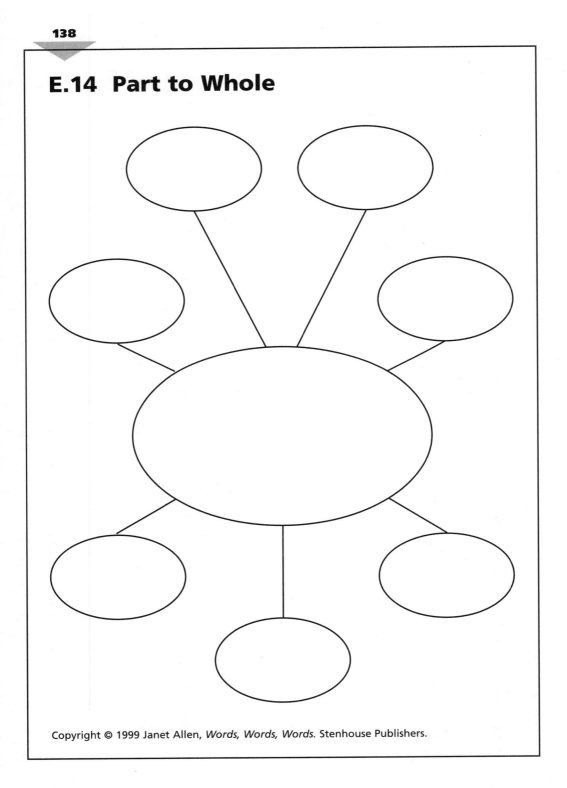

E.15 Words in Context

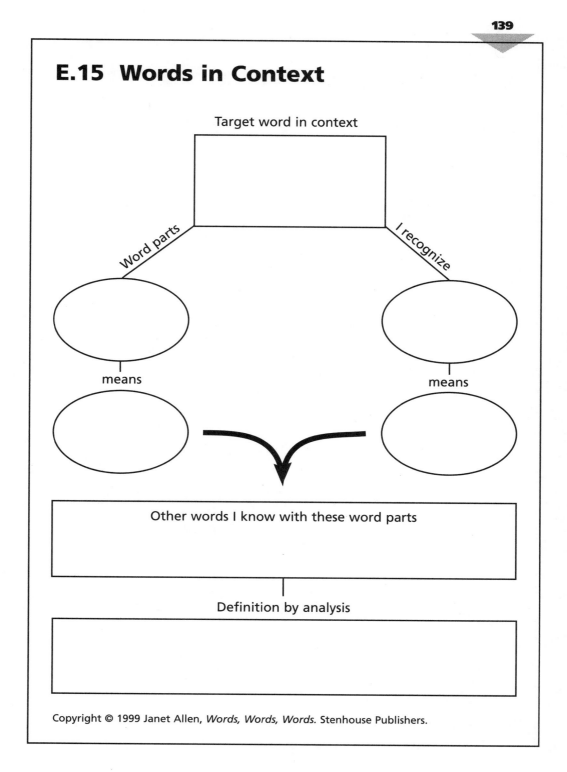

Target word in context

Word parts

I recognize

means

means

Other words I know with these word parts

Definition by analysis

E.16 Words in Context

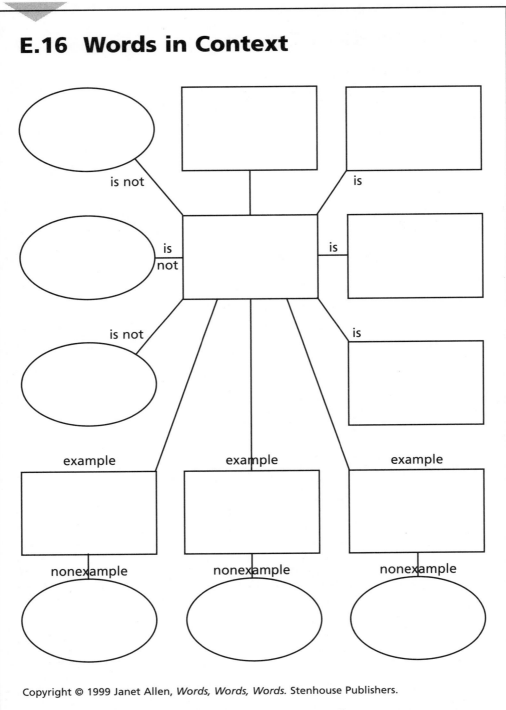

is not

is

is
not

is

is not

is

example

example

example

nonexample

nonexample

nonexample

E.17 Word Questioning

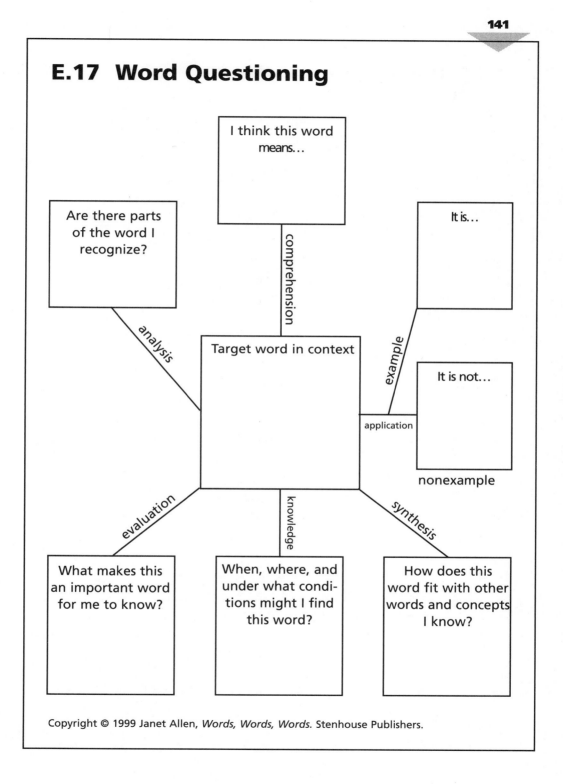

I think this word means...

Are there parts of the word I recognize?

comprehension

analysis

Target word in context

It is...

example

It is not...

application

nonexample

evaluation

knowledge

synthesis

What makes this an important word for me to know?

When, where, and under what conditions might I find this word?

How does this word fit with other words and concepts I know?

Copyright © 1999 Janet Allen, *Words, Words, Words*. Stenhouse Publishers.

E.18 Making Connections

Target word

Context

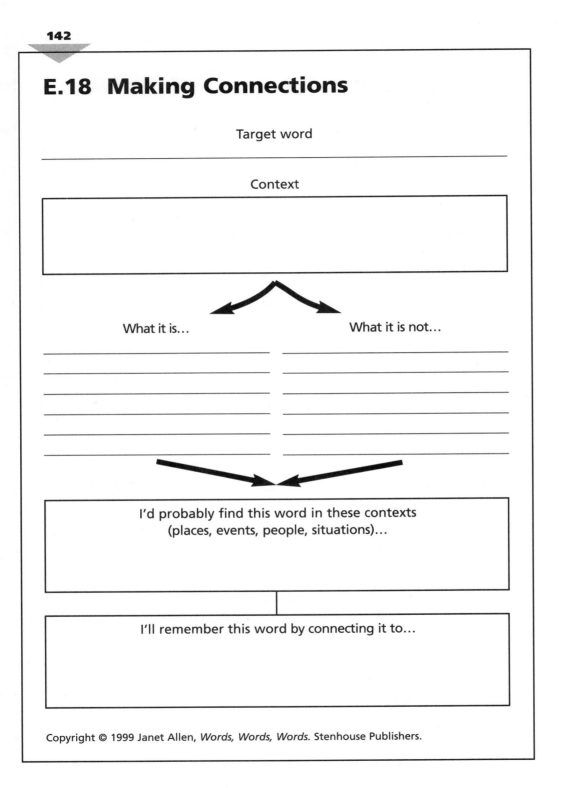

What it is...   What it is not...

I'd probably find this word in these contexts
(places, events, people, situations)...

I'll remember this word by connecting it to...

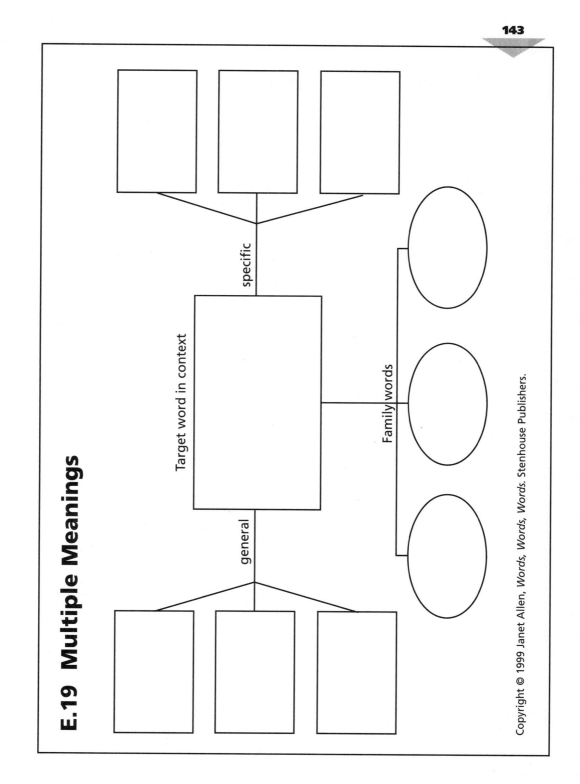

E.19 Multiple Meanings

specific

Target word in context

general

Family words

E.20 Sensory Language Chart

Sight		

Sound		

Smell		

Taste		

Touch		

E.21 Thinking Trees
(Kirby and Kuykendall 1991)

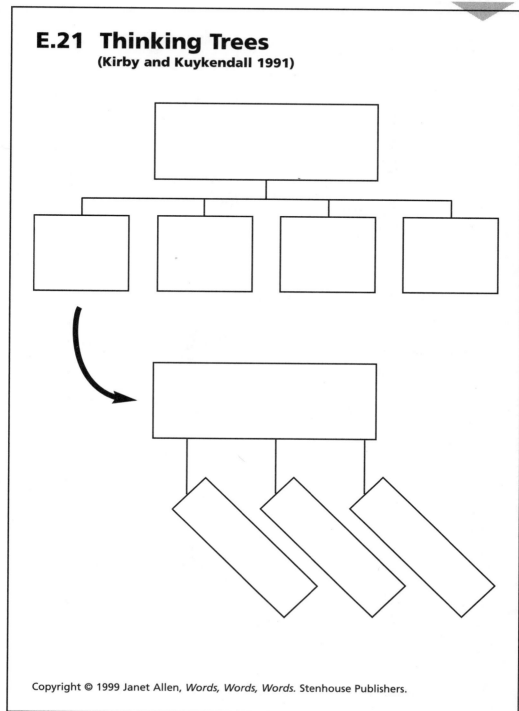

E.22 Word Jars

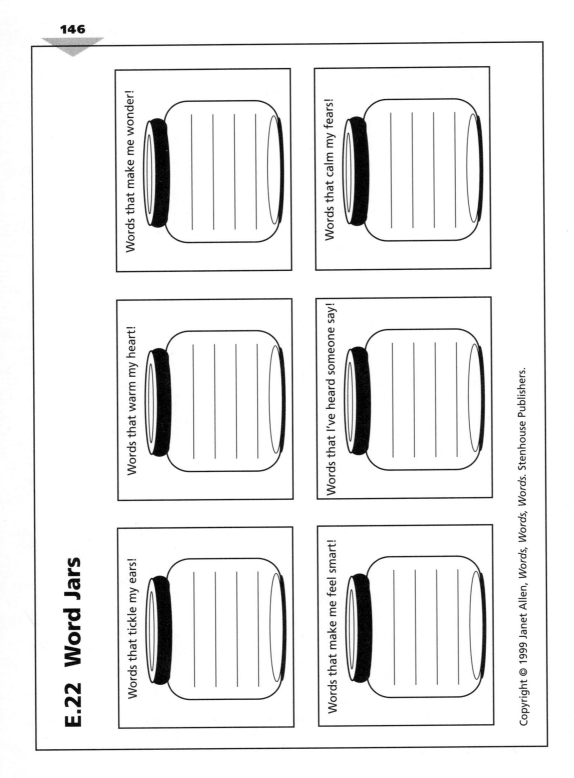

Words that tickle my ears!

Words that warm my heart!

Words that make me wonder!

Words that make me feel smart!

Words that I've heard someone say!

Words that calm my fears!

Professional References

Adams, D., and C. Cerqui. 1989. *Effective Vocabulary Instruction.* Kirkland, WA: Reading Resources.

Allen, J. 1995. *It's Never Too Late: Leading Adolescents to Lifelong Literacy.* Portsmouth, NH: Heinemann

Allen, J., and K. Gonzalez. 1998. *There's Room for Me Here: Literacy Workshop in the Middle School.* York, ME: Stenhouse.

Anderson, R., and W. Nagy. 1991. "Word Meanings." In R. Barr, M. Kamil, P. Monsenthal, and P. D. Pearson, eds., *Handbook of Reading Research,* Vol. 2, pp. 690–724. New York: Longman.

Anderson, R. C., P. T. Wilson, and L. G. Fielding. 1986. *Growth in Reading and How Children Spend Their Time Outside of School.* Technical Report No. 389. Urbana, IL: University of Illinois, Center for the Study of Reading.

Atwell, Nancie. 1998. *In the Middle: New Understandings About Writing, Reading, and Learning.* Portsmouth, NH: Heinemann-Boynton/Cook.

Baker, S. K., D. C. Simmons, and E. J. Kameenui. 1995a. *Vocabulary Acquisition: Curricular and Instructional Implications for Diverse Learners.* Technical Report No. 13. University of Oregon: National Center to Improve the Tools for Educators.

———. 1995b. *Vocabulary Acquisition: Synthesis of the Research.* Technical Report No. 13. University of Oregon: National Center to Improve the Tools for Educators.

Baumann, J. F., and E. J. Kameenui. 1991. "Research on Vocabulary Instruction: Ode to Voltaire." In J. Flood, J. M. Jensen, D. Lapp, and J. R. Squire, eds., *Handbook on Teaching the English Language Arts,* pp. 604–32.

Beck, I. L., E. S. McCaslin, and M. G. McKeown. 1980. *The Rationale and Design of a Program to Teach Vocabulary to Fourth-Grade Students.* (ERDC Publication 1980/25). Pittsburgh University—Pittsburgh Learning Research and Development Center.

Becker, W. C. 1977. "Teaching Reading and Language to the Disadvantaged: What We Have Learned from Field Research." *Harvard Education Review* 47, 518–43.

Beers, K., and B. Samuels, eds. 1998. *Into Focus: Understanding and Creating Middle School Readers.* Norwood, MA: Christopher Gordon.

Blachowicz, C. L. Z. 1986. "Making Connections: Alternatives to the Vocabulary Notebook." *Journal of Reading* 29, 2: 643–49.

Bloom, B., and D. Krathwohl. 1984. *Taxonomy of Educational Objectives: Handbook 1: Cognitive Domain.* Menlo Park, CA: Addison-Wesley.

Caine, R., and G. Caine. 1994. *Making Connections: Teaching and the Human Brain.* Reading, MA: Addison-Wesley.

Carey, S. 1978. "The Child as Word Learner." In M. Hallen, J. Bresnan, and G. Miller, eds., *Linguistic Theory and Psychological Reality.* Cambridge, MA: MIT Press.

Christenbury, L., and P. Kelly. 1983. *Questioning: A Path to Critical Thinking.* Urbana, IL: National Council of Teachers of English.

Coles, R. 1989. *The Call of Stories: Teaching and the Moral Imagination.* Boston: Houghton Mifflin.

Davis, F. B. 1944. "Fundamental Factors in Reading Comprehension." *Psychometrika* 9, 185–97.

———. 1968. "Research on Comprehension in Reading." *Reading Research Quarterly* 3, 499–545.

Freeman, E., and D. Person. 1992. *Using Nonfiction Trade Books in the Elementary Classroom: From Ants to Zeppelins.* Urbana, IL: National Council of Teachers of English.

Freire, P., and D. Macedo. 1987. *Literacy: Reading the Word and the World.* South Hadley, MA: Bergin & Garvey.

Gillet, J. W., and C. Temple. 1982. *Understanding Reading Problems: Assessment and Instruction.* Boston: Little, Brown.

Graves, M., and B. Graves. 1994. *Scaffolding Reading Experiences: Designs for Student Success.* Norwood, MA: Christopher Gordon.

Green, J. 1993. *The Word Wall: Teaching Vocabulary Through Immersion.* Ontario: Pippin.

Heath, S. B., and L. Mangiola. 1991. *Children of Promise: Literate Activity in Linguistically and Culturally Diverse Classrooms.* National Education Association.

Jones, R. 1993. "Generation: An Exercise in AIDS Awareness." *The Science Teacher,* November, 34–41.

Kameenui, E. J. et al. 1982.

Kirby, D., and C. Kuykendall. 1991. *Mind Matters: Teaching for Thinking.* Portsmouth, NH: Heinemann–Boynton/Cook.

Mason, L., J. Garcia, F. Powell, and C. F. Risinger. 1995. *America's Past and Promise.* Evanston, IL: McDougall Little/Houghton Mifflin.

McKeown, M. G., I. L. Beck. 1988. "Learning Vocabulary, Different Ways for Different Goals." *Remedial and Special Education* 9, 16.

McKeown, M. G., I. L. Beck, R. Omanson, and M. T. Pople. 1985. "Some Effects of the Nature and Frequency of Vocabulary Instruction on Reading Comprehension: A Replication." *Journal of Reading Behavior* 15, 3–18.

Meek, M. 1988. *How Texts Teach What Readers Learn.* Great Britain: The Thimble Press.

Milner, J. O., and L. F. M. Milner. 1993. *Bridging English.* New York: Macmillan.

Moffett, J., and B. J. Wagner. 1992. *Student-Centered Language Arts K–12,* Fourth Edition. Portsmouth, NH: Heinemann–Boynton/Cook.

Mooney, M. 1990. *Reading to, with and by Children.* Katonah, NY: Richard C. Owen.

Nagy, W. 1988. *Teaching Vocabulary to Improve Reading Comprehension.* Newark, DE: International Reading Association.

Nagy, W., P. Herman, and R. Anderson. 1985. "Learning Words from Context." *Reading Research Quarterly* 85 Winter, 233–53.

Nagy, W., R. C. Anderson, and R. Herman. 1987. "Learning Word Meanings from Context During Normal Reading." *American Educational Research Journal* 24, 237–70.

Norton, D. 1999. *Through the Eyes of a Child: An Introduction to Children's Literature,* Fifth Edition. New York: Simon & Schuster.

Ohanian, S. 1995. *Ask Ms. Class.* York, ME: Stenhouse.

Reading Today. 1998. (October/November) 16, 2: 12.

Simpson, M. 1962. *Reading in Junior Classes.* Katonah, NY: Richard C. Owen.

Stahl, S., and M. Fairbanks. 1986. "The Effects of Vocabulary Instruction: A Model-Based Meta-Analysis." *Review of Educational Research* 56, 721–810.

Sutherland, Z., and M. H. Arbuthnot. 1991. *Children and Books,* Eighth Edition. New York: HarperCollins.

Taba, H. 1967. *Teacher's Handbook for Elementary Social Studies.* Reading, MA: Addison-Wesley.

Vacca, R. T., and J. L. Vacca. 1986. *Content Area Reading.* Boston: Little, Brown.

Wallis, C. 1998. "How to Make a Better Student." *Time*, October 19, 1998, 78–86.

Will, G. 1998. "The Last Word: It's Outa Here: 60–62" *Newsweek*, March 30, 1998, 76.

Zemelman, S., H. Daniels, and A. Hyde. 1993. *Best Practice: New Standards for Teaching and Learning in America's Schools.* Portsmouth, NH: Heinemann.

Literature References

Agard, John, and Grace Nichols, eds. 1990. *A Caribbean Dozen: Poems from Caribbean Poets.* Cambridge, MA: Candlewick.

Anno, Mitsumasa. 1982. *Anno's Math Games.* New York: Philomel.

———. 1983. *Anno's Mysterious Multiplying Jar.* New York: Philomel.

———. 1986. *Socrates and the Three Little Pigs.* New York: Philomel.

———. 1993. *Anno's Hat Tricks.* New York: Philomel.

———. 1995. *Anno's Magic Seeds.* New York: Philomel.

Arnold, Nick. 1996. *Ugly Bugs.* New York: Scholastic.

Arrick, F. 1994. *What You Don't Know Can Kill You.* New York: Bantam Doubleday Dell.

Barry, David. 1994. *The Rajah's Rice: A Mathematical Folktale from India.* New York: Freeman.

Bloor, Edward. 1997. *Tangerine.* Orlando, FL: Harcourt Brace.

Bode, Janet. 1993. *Death Is Hard to Live With: Teenagers Talk About How They Cope with Loss.* New York: Bantam Doubleday Dell.

———. 1995. *Trust and Betrayal: Real Life Stories of Friends and Enemies.* New York: Bantam Doubleday Dell.

Bode, Janet, and S. Mack. 1996. *Hard Time: A Real-Life Look at Juvenile Crime and Violence.* New York: Bantam Doubleday Dell.

———. 1998. *Vacabutoons, Vocabulary Cartoons: Elementary Edition.* Punta Gorda, FL: New Monic Books.

Bray, Rosemary. 1995. *Martin Luther King, Jr.* New York: Greenwillow.

Brecker, Erwin. 1994. *Lateral Logic Puzzles.* New York: Sterling.

Burchers, Sam, Max Burchers, and Bryan Burchers. 1997. *Vacabutoons, Vocabulary Cartoons: SAT Word Power.* Punta Gorda, FL: New Monic Books.

Campbell, R. No date. "Heading Home." *READ Magazine.* Middleton, CT.

Carlson, Lori, ed. 1994. *Cool Salsa: Bilingual Poems on Growing Up Latino in the United States.* New York: Henry Holt.

Carroll, Lewis. 1946. *Through the Looking Glass.* New York: Grosset and Dunlap.

Christopher, John. 1989. *The White Mountains.* New York: Aladdin Paperbacks.

CityKids Foundation. 1994. *CityKids Speak on Prejudice.* New York: Random House.

Coles, Robert. 1995. *The Story of Ruby Bridges.* New York: Scholastic.

Crutcher, Chris. 1989. *Athletic Shorts.* New York: Bantam Doubleday Dell.

Deary, Terry. 1994. *Horrible Histories: The Rotten Romans.* New York: Scholastic.

———. 1996. *Horrible Histories: The Measly Middle Ages.* New York: Scholastic.

DeGross, M. 1994. *Donovan's Word Jar.* New York: HarperCollins.

Edwards, C., ed. 1995. *Perspectives on History Series: The New Deal: Hope for the Nation.* Carlisle, MA: Discovery Enterprises.

Elster, Charles Harrington, and Joseph Elliot. 1994. *Tooth and Nail: A Novel Approach to the New SAT.* Orlando, FL: Harcourt Brace.

Evans, Nicholas. 1995. *The Horse Whisperer.* New York: Dell.

Feldman, David. 1988. *Why Do Clocks Run Clockwise? and Other Imponderables.* New York: Harper & Row.

———. 1989. *Who Put the Butter in Butterfly? and Other Fearless Investigations into Our Illogical Language.* New York: Harper & Row.

———. 1990. *When Do Fish Sleep? and Other Imponderables of Everyday Life.* New York: HarperCollins.

Fleischman, Paul. 1985. *I Am Phoenix: Poems for Two Voices.* New York: Harper & Row.

———. 1988. *Joyful Noise: Poems for Two Voices.* New York: Harper & Row.

Florian, Douglas. 1998. *Insectlopedia.* Orlando, FL: Harcourt Brace.

Ford, Michael Thomas. 1995. *The Voices of AIDS: Twelve Unforgettable People Talk About How AIDS Has Changed Their Lives.* New York: William Morrow.

Fredericks, Anthony. 1996. *Simple Nature Experiments with Everyday Materials.* New York: Sterling.

Freedman, Russell. 1983. *Children of the Wild West.* New York: Scholastic.

———. 1988. *Buffalo Hunt.* New York: Holiday House.

———. 1992. *An Indian Winter.* New York: Scholastic.

Funk, C. S., and C. S. Funk, Jr. 1986. *Horsefeathers and Other Curious Words.* New York: Harper & Row.

Gallo, Donald. 1995. *Ultimate Sports: Short Stories by Outstanding Writers for Young Adults.* New York: Bantam Doubleday Dell.

Gillette, J. Lynett. 1997. *Dinosaur Ghosts: The Mystery of Coelophysis.* New York: Scholastic.

Goldwyn, Martin. 1979. *How a Fly Walks Upside Down and Other Curious Facts.* New York: Random House.

Gordon, Karen Elizabeth. 1993. *The Deluxe Transitive Vampire: The Ultimate Handbook of Grammar for the Innocent, the Eager, and the Doomed.* New York: Random House.

———. 1993. *The New Well-Tempered Sentence: A Punctuation Handbook for the Innocent, the Eager, and the Doomed.* Boston: Houghton Mifflin.

Gwynne, Fred. 1980. *The Sixteen-Hand Horse.* New York: Simon & Schuster.

———. 1988a. *A Chocolate Moose for Dinner.* New York: Simon & Schuster.

———. 1988b. *The King Who Rained.* New York: Simon & Schuster.

———. 1988c. *A Little Pigeon Toad.* New York: Simon & Schuster.

Haddix, M. 1996. *Don't You Dare Read This, Mrs. Dunphrey.* New York: Aladdin.

Hatch, Thomas. 1997. *Science Court Investigations: Gravity.* Frank Schaffer.

Hausman, Gerald. 1994. *Turtle Island ABC.* New York: HarperCollins.

Heller, Ruth. 1987. *A Cache of Jewels and Other Collective Nouns.* New York: Grosset and Dunlap.

———. 1988. *Kites Sail High: A Book About Verbs.* New York: Grosset and Dunlap.

———. 1990. *Merry-Go-Round: A Book About Nouns.* New York: Grosset and Dunlap.

———. 1997. *Mine, All Mine: A Book About Pronouns.* New York: Scholastic.

Hill, Wayne F., and Cynthia J. Ottchen. 1991. *Shakespeare's Insults: Educating Your Wit.* Miami: MainSail.

———. 1995. *William's Wit Kit.* Miami: MainSail.

Hinton, S. E. 1967. *The Outsiders.* New York: Viking.

Hoffman, Paul. 1998. *The Man Who Loved Only Numbers: The Story of Paul Erdos and the Search for Mathematical Truth.* New York: Hyperion.

Hollander, Zander, ed. 1995. *The NBA Book of Fantastic Facts, Feats, and Super Stats.* New York: Troll.

Howe, James. 1997. *The Watcher.* New York: Simon & Schuster.

Hunt, Irene. 1986. *No Promises in the Wind.* New York: Berkley.

Hunter, Sara Hoagland. 1996. *The Unbreakable Code.* Flagstaff, AZ: Northland.

Ianelli, Richard. 1983. *The Devil's New Dictionary: Diabolic Definitions for Our Times.* Secaucus, NJ: Citadel.

Isdell, Wendy. 1993. *A Gebra Named Al.* Minneapolis, MN: Free Spirit.

———. 1996. *The Chemy Called Al.* Minneapolis, MN: Free Spirit.

Jacobson, John D. 1993. *Eatioms: A Savory Salmagundi of Phrases, Metaphors, and Bon Mots That Are Irresistible Food for Thought.* New York: Dell.

Janeczko, Paul. 1994. *Loads of Codes and Secret Ciphers.* New York: Macmillan.

Johnstone, Michael. 1997. *The History News: Explorers.* New York: Scholastic.

Juster, Norton, and Eric Carle. 1982. *Otter Nonsense.* New York: Putnam.

Kalman, Bobbie. 1994. *Historic Communities: Settler Sayings.* New York: Crabtree.

———. 1995. *Historic Communities: Games from Long Ago.* New York: Crabtree.

Kalman, Bobbie, and Tammy Everts. 1994. *Historic Communities: Customs and Traditions.* New York: Crabtree.

Kalman, Bobbie, and David Schimpky. 1995. *Historic Communities: Children's Clothing of the 1800s.* New York: Crabtree.

Kipling, Rudyard. 1983. *How the Alphabet Was Made.* New York: Macmillan.

Knight, Margy Burns. 1992. *Talking Walls.* Gardiner, ME: Tilbury House.

———. 1993. *Who Belongs Here? An American Story.* Gardiner, ME: Tilbury House.

Kohl, Herbert. 1981. *The Book of Puzzlements: Play and Invention with Language.* New York: Random House.

Konigsburg, Elizabeth. 1987. *From the Mixed-Up Files of Mrs. Basil E. Frankweiler.* New York: Aladdin.

Krull, Kathleen. 1993. *Lives of the Musicians: Good Times, Bad Times, and What the Neighbors Thought.* Orlando, FL: Harcourt Brace.

———. 1994. *Lives of the Writers: Comedies, Tragedies, and what the Neighbors Thought.* Orlando, FL: Harcourt Brace.

———. 1995. *Lives of the Artists: Masterpieces, Messes, and What the Neighbors Thought.* Orlando, FL: Harcourt Brace.

———. 1997. *Lives of the Athletes: Thrills, Spills and What the Neighbors Thought.* Orlando, FL: Harcourt Brace.

Kuklin, Susan. 1993. *Speaking Out: Teenagers Take on Race, Sex, and Identity.* New York: The Putnam and Grosset Group

Kulpa, Kathryn. 1995. *Short Takes: Brief Personal Narratives and Other Works by American Teen Writers.* East Greenwich, RI: Merlin's Pen.

Lasky, Kathryn. 1998. *True North.* New York: Scholastic.

Lederer, Richard. 1987. *Anguished English: An Anthology of Accidental Assaults upon Our Language.* Charleston, SC: Wyrick.

———. 1988. *Get Thee to a Punnery.* Charleston, SC: Wyrick.

———. 1990. *Crazy English: The Ultimate Joy Ride Through Our Language.* New York: Simon & Schuster.

Lederer, Richard, and M. Gilleland. 1994. *Literary Trivia: Fun and Games for Book Lovers.* New York: Random House.

Levey, Judith, ed. 1997. *The World Almanac for Kids 1998.* Mahwah, NJ: Reference Corp.

Levine, Ellen, ed. 1993. *Freedom's Children: Young Civil Rights Activists Tell Their Own Stories.* New York: Avon.

Levitt, Paul, Douglas Burger, and Elissa Guralnick. 1985. *The Weighty Word Book.* Boulder, CO: Bookmakers Guild.

Levy, Elizabeth. 1992. *If You Were There When They Signed the Constitution.* New York: Scholastic.

Loeschnig, Louis. 1997. *Simple Earth Science Experiments*. New York: Sterling.

Lowry, Lois. 1994. *The Giver*. New York: Dell.

Macaulay, David. 1973. *Cathedral*. New York: Trumpet Club.

———. 1975. *Pyramid*. New York: Trumpet Club.

———. 1977. *Castle*. New York: Trumpet Club

———. 1988. *The Way Things Work*. Boston: Houghton Mifflin.

———. 1993. *Ship*. New York: Trumpet Club.

Maestro, Giulio. 1986. *What's Mite Might? Homophone Riddles to Boost Your Word Power!* Boston: Houghton Mifflin.

Magel, John. 1985. *Dr. Moggle's Alphabet Challenge: A Quest for All Ages*. New York: Rand McNally.

Maizels, Jennie, and Kate Petty. 1996. *The Amazing Pop-Up Grammar Book*. New York: Penguin.

Mandell, M. 1993. *Simple Kitchen Experiments: Learning Science with Everyday Foods*. New York: Sterling.

Martin Jr., Bill. 1970. *The Maestro Plays*. New York: Henry Holt.

McGovern, Ann. 1991. *If You Sailed on the Mayflower in 1620*. New York: Scholastic.

McMillan, Bruce, and Brett McMillan. 1982. *Puniddles*. Boston: Houghton Mifflin.

Meltzer, Milton. 1984. *A Book About Names: In Which Custom, Tradition, Law, Myth, History, Folklore, Foolery, Legend, Fashion, Nonsense, Symbol, Taboo Help Explain How We Got Our Names and What They Mean*. New York: HarperCollins.

———. 1992. *The Amazing Potato: A Story in Which the Incas, Conquistadors, Marie Antoinette, Thomas Jefferson, Wars, Famines, Immigrants, and French Fries All Play a Part*. New York: HarperCollins.

———. 1994. *Cheap Raw Material: How Our Youngest Workers Are Exploited and Abused*. New York: Viking.

Miller, Arthur. 1955. *The Crucible*. New York: Penguin.

Miller, William. 1995. *Frederick Douglass: The Last Day of Slavery*. New York: Lee & Low.

Mooney, B. 1997. *The Voices of Silence*. New York: Laurel Leaf.

Moore, Kay. 1997. *If You Lived at the Time of the American Revolution*. New York: Scholastic.

Morris, Deborah. 1997. *Real Kids, Real Adventures: Amazing True Stories of Young Heroes and Survivors Who Lived to Tell the Tale!* New York: Putnam.

Murphy, Jim. 1995. *The Great Fire*. New York: Scholastic.

———. 1996. *A Young Patriot: The American Revolution as Experienced by One Boy*. New York: Scholastic.

Murrow, Liza Ketchum. 1995. *Twelve Days in August*. New York: Avon Books.

Nasar, Sylvia. 1998. *A Beautiful Mind*. New York: Simon & Schuster.

Neuschwander, Cindy. 1997. *Sir Cumference and the First Round Table: A Math Adventure*. New York: Scholastic.

Parker, Steve. 1993. *Brain Surgery for Beginners and Other Major Operations for Minors: A Scalpel-Free Guide to Your Insides*. New York: Scholastic.

Pappas, Theoni. 1991. *Math Talk: Mathematical Ideas in Poems for Two Voices*. San Carlos, CA: Wide World.

Paulos, Martha. 1994. *Insectasides: Great Poets on Man's Pest Friend*. New York: Viking Penguin.

Philbrick, Rodman. 1993. *Freak the Mighty*. New York: Scholastic.

Poortvliet, Rien. 1988. *The Book of the Sandman and the Alphabet of Sleep*. New York: Harry Abrams.

Powell, Anton, and Philip Steele. 1996. *The Greek News: The Greatest Newspaper in Civilization*. Cambridge, MA: Candlewick.

Raboff, Ernest. 1982. *Art for Children: Pablo Picasso*. New York: HarperTrophy.

———. 1987. *Art for Children: Rembrandt.* New York: HarperTrophy.

———. 1987. *Art for Children: Pierre-Auguste Renoir.* New York: HarperTrophy.

———. 1987. *Art for Children: Leonardo Da Vinci.* New York: HarperTrophy.

———. 1988. *Art for Children: Henri Matisse.* New York: HarperTrophy.

Rees, Nigel. 1991. *The Phrase That Launched 1,000 Ships.* New York: Dell.

Ross, Stewart. 1995. *Fact or Fiction: Bandits and Outlaws.* Brookfield, CT: Millbrook.

———. 1995. *Fact or Fiction: Cowboys.* Brookfield, CT: Millbrook.

———. 1995. *Fact or Fiction: Spies and Traitors.* Brookfield, CT: Millbrook.

———. 1996. *Fact or Fiction: Conquerors and Explorers.* Brookfield, CT: Millbrook.

Schechter, Bruce. 1998. *My Brain Is Open.* New York: Simon & Schuster.

Scholastic Voyages. 1995. *The World of Theater.* New York: Scholastic.

Schulman, L. M., ed. 1990. *The Random House Book of Sports Stories.* New York: .

Schwartz, Alvin. 1976. *Kickle Snifters and Other Fearsome Critters Collected from American Folklore.* New York: HarperCollins.

Scieszka, Jon, and Lane Smith. 1995. *Math Curse.* New York: Penguin.

Sloan, Paul. 1992. *Lateral Thinking Puzzlers.* New York: Sterling.

———. 1994. *Test Your Lateral Thinking.* New York: Sterling.

———. 1997. *Perplexing Lateral Thinking Puzzles.* New York: Sterling.

Sloan, Paul, and Des MacHale. 1996. *The Lateral Logician.* New York: Sterling.

Smith, Geof. 1997. *Above 95th Street and Other Basketball Stories.* Los Angeles: Lowell House.

Solomon, Norman. 1992. *The Power of Babble: The Politician's Dictionary of Buzzwords and Double-Talk for Every Occasion.* New York: Dell.

Sparks, Beatrice, ed. 1994. *It Happened to Nancy.* New York: Avon Flare.

Sports Illustrated for Kids. Numerous volumes. New York: Trumpet Club.

Sports Illustrated for Kids. New York: Time.

Stanley, Diane. 1994. *Cleopatra.* New York: William Morrow.

Stanley, Diane, and Peter Vennema. 1992. *Bard of Avon: The Story of William Shakespeare.* New York: William Morrow.

———. 1993. *Charles Dickens: The Man Who Had Great Expectations.* New York: William Morrow.

Steedman, Scott. 1997. *The Egyptian News.* Cambridge, MA: Candlewick.

Steig, Jeanne, and William Steig. 1992. *Alpha Beta Chowder.* New York: HarperCollins.

Steig, William. 1968. *CDB!* New York: Trumpet.

Strasser, Todd. 1998. *Kids' Book of Gross Facts and Feats.* New York: Watermill.

Suid, Murray. 1981. *Demonic Mnemonics.* New York: Dell.

Sweeney, Caroline. 1993. *The Tiger Orchard.* New York: Bantam Doubleday Dell Books for Young Readers.

Tamar, E. 1993. *Fair Game.* Orlando, FL: Harcourt Brace.

Time Machine: An American History Magazine for Kids. Washington, DC: National Museum of American History/Smithsonian Institution.

Van Allsburg, Chris. 1985. *The Polar Express.* Boston: Houghton Mifflin.

Venezia, Mike. 1988. *Getting to Know the World's Greatest Artists: Van Gogh.* Chicago: Children's Press.

———. 1989. *Getting to Know the World's Greatest Artists: Da Vinci.* Chicago: Children's Press.

Viorst, Judith. 1994. *The Alphabet from Z to A.* New York: Macmillan.

Wiesner, David. 1991. *Tuesday.* New York: Clarion.

Wilks, Mike. 1986. *The Ultimate Alphabet.* New York: Henry Holt

———. 1988. *The Annotated Ultimate Alphabet.* New York: Henry Holt

Willard, N. 1990. *The High Rise Glorious Skittle Skat Roarious Sky Pie Angel Food Cake.* Orlando,

FL: Harcourt Brace.

Young, Ed. 1997. *Voices of the Heart.* New York: Scholastic.

Young, Ruth, and Mitchell Rose. 1985. *To Grill a Mockingbird and Other Tasty Titles.* New York: Penguin.

Zhensun, Zheng, and Alice Low. 1991. *A Young Painter: The Life and Paintings of Wang Yani—China's Extraordinary Young Artist.* New York: Scholastic.

Zim, Herbert Spencer. 1997. "owls." In *Elements of Literature, Introductory Course.* New York: Henry Holt.